A BOOK ON

Casino Craps,

Other Dice Games & Gambling Systems

A BOOK ON

Casino Craps,

Other Dice Games & Gambling Systems

C. Ionescu Tulcea

Professor of Mathematics
Northwestern University

VNR **VAN NOSTRAND REINHOLD COMPANY**
NEW YORK   CINCINNATI   ATLANTA   DALLAS   SAN FRANCISCO
LONDON   TORONTO   MELBOURNE

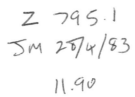

Van Nostrand Reinhold Company Regional Offices:
New York Cincinnati Atlanta Dallas San Francisco

Van Nostrand Reinhold Company International Offices:
London Toronto Melbourne

Copyright © 1981 by Litton Educational Publishing, Inc.

Library of Congress Catalog Card Number: 80-17375
ISBN: 0-442-26713-4
ISBN: 0-442-25725-2 pbk.

Manufactured in the United States of America

Published by Van Nostrand Reinhold Company
135 West 50th Street, New York, N.Y. 10020

Published simultaneously in Canada by Van Nostrand Reinhold Ltd.

15 14 13 12 11 10 9 8 7 6 5 4 3 2 1

Library of Congress Cataloging in Publication Data

Ionescu Tulcea, Cassius, 1923–
    A book on casino craps, other dice games, and
gambling systems.

    Bibliography: p.
    Includes index.
    1. Dice. 2. Craps (Game) 3. Gambling systems.
I. Title.
GV1303.I66   795.1   80-17375
ISBN 0-442-26713-4
ISBN 0-442-25725-2 (pbk.)

Preface

A Book on Casino Craps discusses Casino dice games, several other dice games, and various gambling systems. The book has been written for the general public. It does not assume any gambling or mathematical knowledge on the part of the reader.

The book is divided into three chapters. Chapter 1 discusses the Casino game of Craps as played in Nevada, Atlantic City, England, and other parts of the world. Among the types of bets mentioned are the various Odds bets, methods of hedging bets, and bets combining Pass line bets and Place bets. The best bets a player can make are indicated. The chapter contains a historical note and a section on cheating in dice games.

The first chapter includes a section on probabilities and fair payoffs in the game of Craps. We introduce this section here since many players will want to know the probabilities of winning certain bets and the corresponding fair payoffs. This section is especially important for players who participate in the private game of Craps as it might bring them substantial gains.

In Chapter 2, we describe more than 20 dice games. Special attention is given to the Private game of Craps, in which the variety of bets encountered is far greater than in Casino Craps. The players may make among themselves any type of bets they wish. In the Private game of Craps, the players who have more knowledge of the probabilities and fair payoffs of the possible bets have a substantial advantage over the players who have less knowledge.

Among the other games presented in this chapter is the Two-dice Hazard, which is generally considered to be the ancestor of modern Craps. The discussion of this game here is far more complete than any in the existing literature. Several of the games described in this chapter are new and could make interesting Casino games. Several other games—for instance, Double the sixes—are very deceptive and hence could be profitable to an enterprising person.

In Chapter 3, we make a few remarks concerning probability and expectation. The meaning of percent advantage is explained, and various gambling systems are thoroughly discussed. The gambler's ruin formula and several of its consequences are given. We suggest that every gambler acquire an understanding of these.

The author wishes to express his thanks to the colleagues and friends who made valuable suggestions, especially to Ralph Boas, Eugene Falken, Zita Hayward, Joseph Jerome, and Denis White. The author also thanks Alberta Gordon and Ella Harwood of Van Nostrand Reinhold Company for their assistance in the publication of the book.

Contents

viii   CONTENTS

1. Casino Craps

Craps is one of the two most popular Casino games.* The large variety of possible bets and the direct physical participation of the player are two of the main reasons for its popularity.

Some of the bets which can be placed in this game are, in a certain sense (and if we exclude Blackjack), *the most favorable Casinos offer*. Either directly or indirectly, this must be another reason for the popularity of Craps. We must say, too, that in our opinion the game of Craps is presently the most interesting dice game.

The game of Craps** is played by rolling two dice on a table with a high board and a layout as in Fig. 1. There are small variations in the design of the layout, depending usually on the town you are in. However, once the player becomes familiar with one type of layout, these differences will not cause any difficulties.

The game is conducted by five casino employees, two Boxmen, the Stickman and two Dealers. (Sometimes there is only one Boxman.) These employees are usually positioned as shown in Fig. 1.

The main responsibilities of the Boxmen are to supervise the game. In case of dispute, their decision is final. The Stickman

---

*The other is the game of Blackjack.
**The main purpose of this chapter is to describe completely the game of Craps as played in most Casinos, to discuss the best bets a player may make and to derive the best methods of play. Variants of the game are described in Chapter 2.

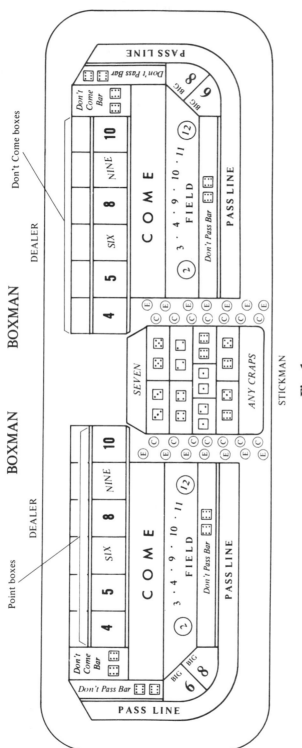

Fig. 1

directs the game. The duties of the two Dealers will become clear during the description of the game.

The number of players at a Craps table is limited only by the space available.

To make bets in the game of Craps (the type of bets which can be placed will be described and discussed below), the player needs chips. They can be bought at the gaming table or, in some places, at the cashier's cage. To buy chips at the table, the player places money in front of one of the two Dealers. The Dealer gives the money to one of the Boxmen, who counts the amount and drops it into the *money box*. Then the Dealer places an equivalent amount in chips in front of the player.

These chips should be removed from the table since they can be mistaken for bets. They may be placed in the grooves found on the boards of the table.

Each Craps table has minimum and maximum limits for the bets a player can make *at that table*. These limits are usually, if not always, prominently displayed. On the Las Vegas Strip, the most usual minimum limits are $1, $2 or $5, while the maximum limits are $500, $1000 or $2000. Although there are Casinos having even lower minimum limits, one will have a hard time finding plush Casinos allowing $1 or even $2 bets.

We also observe that the maximum limit might *not be allowed* for all types of bets; for example, for the high payoff bets described later in this chapter. We shall see, for example, that for a bet on 2 or a bet on 12, the payoff is 29 to 1 (sometimes 30 to 1) in case of a win. A player allowed* to make such a bet for $2000 would receive $58,000 (or $60,000) in case of a win.

HISTORICAL NOTE

How did the game of Craps evolve? Is Craps a modern version of some old game? And when in the past did mankind start to play games of chance?

These are complicated questions. Excavations have produced

---

*There are objective reasons why, in general, Casinos cannot allow such bets.

*astragali** and *dice* from thousands of years before Christ. It will never be possible to determine precisely when mankind started to play games of chance. It is thought, however, that astragali and dice were used for gaming at least 300 years before Christ. Cards were introduced only much later: in Europe, during the fourteenth century; in China, no later than the twelfth century.

To trace relatively precisely the games which led to Craps is probably an impossible task. In any case, most of the students of the history of the game think that either the old game of *Two-dice Hazard* is its direct ancestor, or at least that many features of Craps derived from Hazard. Of course, one can also ask what games Hazard derived from!

As far as the game of Hazard is concerned, one legend says that it was invented in the Middle East and brought to Europe by the Third Crusaders (1189–1192). Once the game was known in Europe, it is not hard to imagine how it later on found its way to America.

Whether or not the game was brought from the Middle East to Europe is not completely clear. If it *was* invented in the Middle East (which is probably true), it must have been brought to Europe earlier than the end of the twelfth century. As M. G. Kendall** observes, references to Hazard in the Western European literature can be found as early as A.D. 1155.

There are difficulties in tracing the beginnings of Craps, undoubtedly because there were several variants of Hazard and it is hard to determine exactly what the old rules were.

The first publications in which one can find complete rules for Two-dice Hazard are *The Compleat Gamester* by Charles Cotton[5] and *Essay d'Analyse sur les Jeux de Hasard* by Pierre Remond de Montmort.[21] Although the rules are described completely in both books, and Cotton's remarks are quite entertain-

---

*The *astragalus* is a bone in the ankle, and is considered as "the ancestor" of dice. Bones from small animals were mainly used.
**See "A note on playing cards," in E. S. Pearson and M. G. Kendall (Eds.), *Studies in the History of Statistics and Probability*, Charles Griffin, London, 1970, pp. 35–36.

ing, de Montmort discusses the game in more detail and his presentation is very clear and almost in modern form. A reader who does not already know the rules of Hazard will have a hard time understanding them from the *Compleat Gamester.**

As far as the name Craps is concerned, notice that the outcomes 2 or 3, which play an essential role in the game of Hazard, were called *Crabs* in England. It is probable that "Craps" derived from "Crabs."

The reader who consults the section on Hazard in Chapter 2 will see how closely this game and Craps are related. In the author's opinion, the two games are indeed closely related and the theory which says that Craps evolved as a simplification of Hazard is acceptable.

The Black American seems to have played an important part in the early stages of this process of simplification. In *Scarne on Dice*,[25] John Scarne gives special credit to John H. Winn for special contributions to Craps. In recent times, John Scarne himself contributed to the game.

Of course, it took a long time and gradual development for the game to arrive at the form in which it is offered nowadays in Casinos.

DICE AND OUTCOMES

Everybody knows what a *die* is, that it has six faces and that each face is marked with from one to six dots. We identify the faces of the die by one of the numbers 1, 2, . . . , 6. For instance, 3 will *identify the face marked by three dots.*

Most dice are marked so that the sum of numbers on *opposite faces* is 7. For instance, if a face is marked by 5, then the opposite one is marked by 2.

The dice at a Craps table are rolled by one of the players participating in the game.

---

*Charles Cotton was aware, for example, that the outcome 7 is produced more often than 6, or than 8. This is quite interesting, especially since he does not determine correctly the number of ways in which 6, 8 and 7 can be obtained.

Assume that a die is rolled (thrown) on a table. If, after the roll, the number facing *upward* is (for instance) 4, we say that we *rolled* (or threw) 4, or that the *outcome* is 4.* Observe that in this case the face sitting on the table is marked by 3.

When we roll an *honest die* on a table, there is no reason to expect that the outcome will be (for instance) 6 instead of 2. The outcomes 1, 2, 3, 4, 5 or 6 are *equally likely*.**

When we *roll two dice*, 36 different outcomes are possible. To understand this, imagine that one of the dice is *green* and the other *red* (at a Craps table both dice have the same color). If we roll the two dice and if, for example, 4 is rolled with the green die and 6 with the red one, we say that we *rolled* or *threw* (4, 6) or that the *outcome* is (4, 6).

Since with each one of the two dice we may roll any one of the numbers 1, 2, 3, 4, 5 or 6, it is obvious that all the possible outcomes are as in Table 1.

Table 1.

(1, 6)	(2, 6)	(3, 6)	(4, 6)	(5, 6)	(6, 6)
(1, 5)	(2, 5)	(3, 5)	(4, 5)	(5, 5)	(6, 5)
(1, 4)	(2, 4)	(3, 4)	(4, 4)	(5, 4)	(6, 4)
(1, 3)	(2, 3)	(3, 3)	(4, 3)	(5, 3)	(6, 3)
(1, 2)	(2, 2)	(3, 2)	(4, 2)	(5, 2)	(6, 2)
(1, 1)	(2, 1)	(3, 1)	(4, 1)	(5, 1)	(6, 1)

It follows that there are 36 possible outcomes. As in the case of one die, these 36 *outcomes are equally likely to occur*.

In the game of Craps, we are not, in general, *directly* con-

---

*Sometimes we shall say that we *produced* or *obtained* 4. The same terms will be used, without further explanation, in similar situations.

**When we toss a coin a large number of times, each one of the two sides (head or tail) will turn up *about half of the time*. We say that the *probability* of the *outcome head* and that of the *outcome tail* are equal to 1/2. When a die is rolled a large number of times, each one of the six faces will turn up about *one-sixth of the time*. We say that the *probability* to roll a given face is 1/6.

In general, *the probability of an event* measures the likelihood of its occurrence. The larger the probability is, the greater the chance of occurrence of the corresponding event.

cerned with the numbers we roll with each one of the two dice, but *with the sum (or total) of these numbers.*

If we have thrown, for example, (2, 6), the corresponding sum, or total, is 8. If we rolled (1, 6) or (6, 1), the sum is the same, namely 7. Of course, the sum, or total, is 7, whenever we roll

$$(1, 6), (6, 1), (2, 5), (5, 2), (4, 3) \text{ or } (3, 4).$$

Assume that we have thrown (3, 5), for example. If we are interested only in the corresponding sum, we shall say that we *rolled* (or *threw*) 8 or that the *outcome* is 8.

To understand why certain bets are more favorable than others, it is necessary to have some idea of the relation between the outcome as a pair of numbers and the outcome as a total.

Table 2 (*which does not have to be memorized by the reader*) indicates which ones of the outcomes are most likely to occur.

Table 2.

2 can be rolled only in one way (namely, (1, 1)).
12 can be rolled only in one way (namely, (6, 6)).
3 and 11 can (each) be rolled only in two ways.
4 and 10 can (each) be rolled only in three ways.
5 and 9 can (each) be rolled only in four ways.
6 and 8 can (each) be rolled only in five ways.
7 can be rolled in *six* ways.

Hence, *when you roll two dice, the outcomes with the least chance to occur are 2 and 12. The outcome having the best chance is 7. The outcomes having the next best chance are 6 and 8.*

The outcome 2 is sometimes called *snake-eyes.* The outcome 12 is called *box-cars.* The outcomes 2, 3 or 12 are called *Craps.*

In the long run, 7 is rolled about one-sixth of the time. The outcome will be 2 about once in 36 rolls. The outcome will be 11 about once in 18 rolls. The outcome will be 12 about once in 36 rolls.

Of course, *for playing well* it is not necessary to remember *why* certain bets are better than others. It is enough just to know which ones of the bets are more favorable to the player. This will be indicated below.

Before we go on, it should be pointed out that while there is no doubt whatsoever that the statements above are true, some of these statements might not be immediately obvious. At least, they were not so in the past.

Consider, for instance, the example of Jean d'Alembert (1717-1783), who left a very rich and important scientific legacy and whose work was not without influence on Probability theory. His name is also related to a certain gambling system we shall discuss in Chapter 3.

In an article written for the first edition of one of the volumes of the famous french "Encyclopédie," D'Alembert examines the probability of producing two heads in two tosses of a coin and concludes *wrongly* that it is 1/3 (we present the reasoning which led to this wrong result in Chapter 3).

We observe that the possible outcomes corresponding to two tosses of a coin are

(tail, tail), (tail, head), (head, head) and (head, tail)

and that these four outcomes are equally likely. Hence, *the probability of obtaining two heads in two tosses of a coin is 1/4.*

WHAT ABOUT LUCK?

In this section, a few remarks will be made concerning dice games and gaming in general. Let us begin with two stories, to be used as the basis for these remarks.

One Sunday afternoon, when we were both about twelve years old, my cousin George and I found several dice in a drawer, in my home. We picked two, "invented" a game and started playing it in the garden. The rules were as follows: We rolled the pair of dice, and when the outcome was 8 my cousin would win; when the outcome was 10 I would win. The other outcomes were ignored. Each time, we bet the same amount, and the payoff corresponding to a win was 1 to 1.

Why I chose 10 for my number, I do not remember. Probably I thought that "bigger was better."

Quickly—very quickly—my cousin won all the money I had in my pocket. In fact, I ended by owing him my next week's allowance.

While neither of us understood *then* why this happened, the reason for George's win was very simple. It can be found by inspecting Table 2: 10 can be produced only in 3 ways, while 8 can be rolled in 5 ways. Hence, the probability of the outcome 8 is greater than that of the outcome 10. In fact, it is almost twice as large. Thus, my cousin had a huge advantage.

The second story concerns a question posed to Galileo Galilei (1564-1642) by an Italian nobleman and gambler. The gambler observed that when you throw *three dice** the total 10 occurs more often than the total 9. He wondered why. Galileo solved the problem by showing that 10 can be obtained in 27 ways, while 9 can be produced in 25 ways only. Hence, the probability of rolling 10 is greater than that of rolling 9, and hence the player betting on 10 had the advantage.

"All right," certain gamblers will say. "We understand that 8 can be produced in more ways than 10, and we also understand that when you roll three dice 10 can be obtained in more ways than 9. But what about *luck*? For example, when you gambled against George, maybe you would have won if you wore a red hat or if at least you had a red handkerchief in your pocket."

What these gamblers should understand is that if you play *long enough*, in any game in which you are at a disadvantage, you will almost certainly lose. There is no doubt about this. In the *long run*, "luck" cannot offset an edge against you.

In the game described in the first story, my cousin's advantage was so huge that it would have been practically impossible to win, even if we had played for only a relatively short time.

In any case, we can end this section on a *positive note*. The

*Here we use some obvious terminology, similar to that introduced in the case when we roll two dice. The reader interested in more details may consult the section on *rolls of three dice* in Chapter 2.

player who has enough capital, and participates in a game that is only slightly unfavorable, * has a considerable chance of winning a "reasonable" amount. What "reasonable" means, and how large the capital should be, will be discussed in Chapter 3.

ROLLS OF DICE AT A CRAPS TABLE: COME-OUT ROLLS AND POINT ROLLS

In the game of Craps, the dice are thrown by one of the players.

The rolls encountered at a Craps table are of two kinds: *come-out rolls* and *point rolls*. To understand the rules of the game, one should know when a throw of the dice is a come-out roll and when it is a point roll.

Assume, for instance, that Ted arrives at a Craps table, where a player is ready to throw the two dice. Will the roll by a come-out roll or a point roll? Ted may learn of what type the roll is by looking at the two large discs (the *point markers*) on the table. These discs are usually white. If the discs are placed clear of *point boxes*, the throw is a *come-out roll*. When the point markers are clear of point boxes, they are usually placed either in the *don't come areas* or close to the chips box.

If the discs are placed in point boxes, the roll is a *point roll*. In fact, these discs are never placed completely inside point boxes; they are positioned as shown in Fig. 2. Also, one only needs to determine where *one* of the two discs is placed. The discs are either both clear of point boxes or both in point boxes (with the same number).

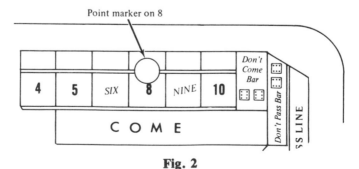

Point marker on 8

Fig. 2

*Like *certain bets* in the game of Craps.

The Stickman will often shout "Coming out" before a come-out roll.

The first roll made by a player arriving at a table where previously there were no players is a come-out roll. Also, every roll following a throw which has an outcome of 7 is a come-out. If 7, 11 or Craps are rolled on a come-out roll, then the next throw is also a come-out.

Other cases when a throw is a come-out roll are indicated below. In any case, the position of the point markers will always tell the arriving player whether the next roll is a come-out or a point roll.

An outcome of 7 or 11 on a come-out roll is called a Natural.

PASS LINE BETS

To make a *pass line bet*, the player places chips in the *pass line area* (see Fig. 3). Such a bet can be placed before any roll of the dice. *The player should remember, however, to place pass line bets only before come-out rolls.* (The reason for this is explained later in this section.)

The great majority of Craps players wager on the pass line.

Assume that John made a pass line bet before a come-out roll.

If the outcome of the roll is 7 or 11 (that is, a Natural), he wins *even money*.*

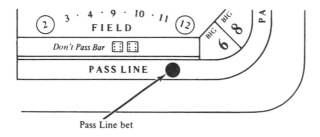

Pass Line bet

Fig. 3

*If, for instance, John bets $10, he wins $10. Hence, he collects a total (his bet included) of $20.

If the outcome of the roll is 2, 3 or 12 (that is, Craps), John loses his bet.

If the outcome is any other number, that is

$$4, 5, 6, 8, 9 \text{ or } 10,$$

then this number becomes *the point*. In this case, the dealer moves the point markers to the corresponding boxes. For instance, if the outcome of the come-out roll is 9, the point markers will be placed in the point boxes marked by the number 9. The dice continue to be rolled (*these rolls are called point rolls*) until the outcome is *either 7 or the point*.

If 7 is rolled *before* the point, John loses his bet. If the point is rolled *before* 7, John wins even money. *Hence, for pass line bettors, 7 is a "good" outcome on come-out rolls and a "bad" outcome on point rolls.*

When the outcome is either 7 or the point, the *next* roll is again a come-out roll.

The payoff, when the player wins with a pass line bet, is made by the dealer placing an equal amount of chips next to the initial bet (see Fig. 4).

The Casino advantage in the case of pass line bets is about 1.41%. This means that, in the long run, John will lose about 1.41% of the total amount of money placed in the pass line area.*

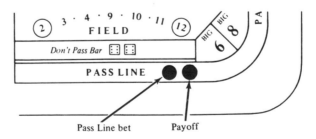

Fig. 4

*The percentages corresponding to the various bets discussed in this volume are computed, in general, with respect to the average amount of money placed on the table. We observe that the smaller the percent advantage of the House is, the better the bet is for the player.

The pass line bet is one of the best bets a player can make in a Casino. In Chapter 3 we shall indicate what chance a player has to win (under certain conditions) a certain amount of dollars. We shall see that the probability of a win of a reasonable amount is considerable if the initial capital is large enough.

As indicated earlier, 7 can be rolled in 6 ways and 11 in 2 ways. Hence, there are 8 ways in which we can produce either 7 or 11. So, on the average, 8 times in 36 throws (or once in 4.5 throws!), the outcome is 7 or 11. Similarly, 2, 3 or 12 can be rolled in 4 ways, so that, on the average, the player wins 8 times in 36 rolls and loses only 4 times in 36 rolls. Therefore, on the come-out roll, the player who makes a pass line bet has an edge over the House. However, once a point is established, it is the House that has the advantage, since 7 will be rolled more often than any other number. And this edge is so substantial that it cancels completely the player's edge on the come-out roll and gives the Casino the overall advantage of 1.4% indicated above.

Summing up the above remarks, we may say that the player has the advantage on come-out rolls and the House on point rolls. This is why the player should not place pass line bets on point rolls, and this is why *the House does not allow the player to remove pass line bets on point rolls.*

One question which is interesting for both Casinos and players, is the following: *How many rolls of the dice are necessary for settling a pass line bet?*

Of course, since there are 12 ways in which one can roll one of the numbers 7, 11, 2, 3 or 12, it follows that one-third of the time the pass line bets will be settled in one throw. On the other hand, one may throw the dice 10 or more times without producing 7 or the point. Before proceeding further, we notice that such an occurrence is far from being as extraordinary an event as it may seem. In any case, instead of continuing with such remarks, we observe that the answer to the question asked above is as follows:

The expected number of rolls of the dice necessary to settle a pass line bet is about 3.37.

This means that, *on the average,* a pass line bet will be settled in about 3.37 rolls (that is, in about 3 or 4 rolls).

One other similar result is the following:

Once a point is established, the expected number of rolls necessary to settle the bet is about 3.56.

This means that once a point is established, the bet will be settled, on the average, in about 3.56 rolls (that is, in about 3 or 4 rolls).

Notice that the average number of rolls necessary for settling a pass line bet is somewhat less than the average number of rolls necessary for settling the bet, *once a point has been established.* If this appears to be contradictory, then we should recall that, on the come-out roll, pass line bets are settled right away about one-third of the time.

Casinos could be interested in certain variants of the game of Craps in which the bets could be settled with fewer throws of the dice, even if such variants would give the House a somewhat smaller percent advantage.

Pass line bets are also called *line bets.* The *dice pass* when the outcomes are such that the *pass line bettors win.* The *dice don't pass* when the outcomes are Craps on come-out rolls and 7 on point rolls.

COME BETS

Players may make pass line bets before any throw of the dice. However, as explained above, such bets should not be placed before point rolls, since in this case the Casino advantage is too great.

If the next roll is a *point roll,* and if a player wants to enter the game right away and make a bet similar to the pass line bet, that player should place a come bet. Such a bet is made by placing chips on the table, in the come area. If you place a come bet before a come-out roll, your bet will be moved (usually) in the pass line area.

Assume that Carol made a come bet.

If the outcome of the next roll is 7 or 11, she wins *even money.*

If the outcome is 2, 3 or 12, Carol loses her bet.

If the outcome is any one of the remaining numbers, say 8, then 8 becomes *the point for Carol's come bet*.* In this case, the Dealer moves her bet to the point box marked by the number 8 (see Fig. 5). The bet remains there until either 7 or 8 is *thrown*. If 7 is rolled *first*, Carol loses her come bet. If 8 is thrown *before* 7, Carol wins *even money*.

We notice that the point for Carol's come bet may be different from the point established by the come-out roll.

If the bet is still in the come area, a win is paid by the Dealer, by placing an equal amount in chips, next to the player's bet. If the bet was moved to a point box, then the Dealer places first an equal amount in chips, next to the bet, and then he moves the total amount to the initial position of the bet, in the come area.

To sum up the above discussion, we may say that a come bet wins and loses the same way as a pass line bet. *The House edge in the case of come bets is the same as in the case of pass line bets* (that is, about 1.41%).

When you place a come bet, don't let it be moved to "the previous point," no matter what that point is. Remember: When you make such a bet, you win if the outcome of the next roll is 7 or 11. Hence, on the next roll, you have the advantage. Only after the point is established (for your come bet), does the House have an advantage.

One day I was watching the game at a Craps table in a major Casino on the Las Vegas strip. A new player with a big cowboy

Carol's Come bet

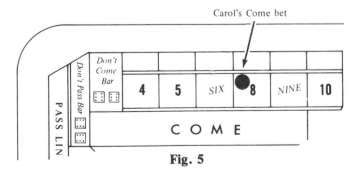

Fig. 5

*The points corresponding to come bets are often called *come points*.

hat entered the game. The point was 5. The player placed a $20 bill in the come bet area. Swiftly, one of the Dealers took the bill, changed it into 4 red $5 chips and placed them in one of the point boxes marked by the number 5. For various reasons, I am certain that this was done on purpose. The outcome of the next roll was 7, and the dealer collected the $20 bet. The $5 chips should have been placed, of course, in the come bet area and the cowboy should have been paid. However, he was not. His (not so loud) protests were of no avail.

You should be careful to make certain that *your chips are placed where you want them to be placed*. If nobody is listening to you, the following procedure is very effective. Place one of your hands on the table. They will tell you to take it off. When they do, ask if your chips are in the right place.

PLACE BETS

Place bets can be made on any of the following numbers:

$$4, 5, 6, 8, 9 \text{ or } 10$$

Notice that these are the numbers marking the point boxes. *A place bet can be made or removed at any time.*

Assume that John wants to make a place bet on 5. For this, he will place the bet (the chips) in one of the positions indicated in Fig. 6.

Since he might be unable to reach the point box 5, John will usually put the chips somewhere on the table and inform one of the Dealers of his intention. The Dealer will then move the chips to the proper place on the layout. In case of a win, the payoff and the initial bet are moved back in front of the player.

The place bet on 5 will remain on the table until either 7 *or* 5 is rolled. If 7 is rolled *first*, John loses the bet. If 5 is rolled *first*, John wins.

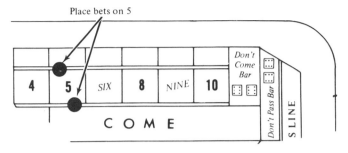

Fig. 6

The other place bets are settled in a similar manner.

The payoffs corresponding to the various place bets depend on the number the bet is placed on:

A place bet on 4 or 10 is paid 9 to 5, in case of a win.

A place bet on 5 or 9 is paid 7 to 5, in case of a win.

A place bet on 6 or 8 is paid 7 to 6, in case of a win.

As far as place bets are concerned, the Casino has the advantage. The edge depends on the number the bet is placed on:

In case of a place bet on 4 or 10, the edge is about 6.7%.

In case of a place bet on 5 or 9, the edge is about 4%.

In case of a place bet on 6 or 8, the edge is about 1.5%.

It follows that, from the player's point of view, the best place bets are those on 6 or 8. In fact, these bets are almost as good as the pass line bets.

If you make place bets on 4, 10, 5 or 9, you should at least place them in multiples of five minimum table bets, since a win might otherwise not be paid correctly. Hence, if you play at a $1-minimum table, you should bet $5, or $10 (10 = 2 × 5), or $15 (15 = 3 × 5), etc. Place bets on 6 or 8 should be made in multiples of six minimum table bets (for the same reason as above). For instance, if you play at a $5-minimum table, you should bet $30, or $60 (60 = 10 × 6), or $90 (90 = 15 × 6), etc.

A bet relatively common (at least in certain Casinos) is the *32-across the board* bet.* This bet is made by placing, at the same time, $5 on each one of the number 4, 5, 9 and 10 and $6 on each one of the numbers 6 and 8.

If a 7 is thrown right away, the player who made a 32-across the board bet will lose $32.

The House advantage in the case of this bet is about 3.9%.

A place bet is off on come-out rolls unless the player requests the contrary. If the player wants the bet *on*, a small *on-disc* is placed on the chips. Of course, it would be simpler if the rules were so that such bets were always on.

PASS LINE AND PLACE BETS

The following method of play, or certain variants of it, is often used at Craps tables: The player starts by placing a pass line bet on a come-out roll. If the shooter rolls a point (for example, a 5), the player takes odds and place bets on *all* numbers (that is, on 4, 5, 6, 8, 9 and 10). Some players make bets only on 6 or 8, presumably since among the numbers marking the point boxes, these two have the best chances of occurrence.

If the shooter will now roll a 7, the player will, of course, lose the pass line bet, the odds and all the place bets. If, for instance, the player's bets were equal to $30, the total loss would be $240.

However, if it takes many throws of the dice to produce the point or 7, the player may win—relatively quickly—substantial amounts. For example, if the shooter rolls

$$4, 12, 3, 8, 6, 2, 9$$

and finally 5, the player wins

$$\$54 + \$35 + \$35 + \$42 + \$42 + \$30 + \$45,$$

that is, $283 (the last two amounts in the above sum correspond to the pass line bets and odds bets, respectively). If the place bet

---

*The author is indebted to Samuel Kotz for suggesting that this bet be described in the text.

on 10 is left on the layout after the shooter rolls 5, the final expected gain is somewhat smaller.

When the player makes place bets only on 6 and 8, the Casino advantage is about 1.1%. The Casino edge is substantially higher when the player makes place bets on all the numbers.

We observe that the House percent advantages given above were computed under the hypothesis that the pass line bets, odds bets and place bets were of equal amount. We also assumed that the odds bets and the place bets were paid correctly. When this is not the case, the results are somewhat different.

DON'T PASS BETS

To make a *don't pass bet*, the player places chips in the *don't pass area* (see fig. 7). Such a bet is allowed only before come-out rolls (the reasons for this will be explained below).

Assume that Gene made a don't pass bet before a come-out roll.

If the outcome is 7 or 11 (that is, a Natural), Gene loses his bet.

If the outcome is 2 or 3, Gene wins *even money*.

If the outcome is 12, he ties.

If the outcome is any other number (that is, 4, 5, 6, 8, 9 or 10), then this number becomes the point. In this case, the Dealer moves the point markers to the corresponding boxes (see the section on pass line bets). The dice continue to be rolled until the outcome is *either 7 or the point*.

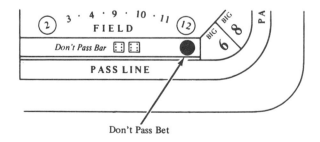

Don't Pass Bet

Fig. 7

If the point is rolled *before* 7, Gene loses his bet. If 7 is rolled *before* the point, he wins even money. *Hence, for don't pass bettors, 7 is a "bad" outcome on come-out rolls and a "good" outcome on point rolls.*

The payoff is made by one of the Dealers by placing an equal amount of chips next to the player's bet.

Since 7 and 11 are produced more often than 2 and 3, the House has the advantage on the come-out roll. Since 7 is produced more often than any given point, it is the player who has the advantage on point rolls. This is why you are not allowed to place don't pass bets before point rolls.

The House advantage in the case of don't pass bets is very close to that in the case of pass line bets. More precisely, it is about 1.36%.

If we recall that the Casino edge in the case of pass line bets is about 1.41%, we conclude that, in a certain sense, don't pass bets are somewhat more advantageous for the player. However, they are only very, very slightly more advantageous. A simple example will help make clear this assertion. Assume that Gene makes, over a certain period, don't pass bets totaling $1,000,000, and that George makes pass line bets also totaling $1,000,000. In this case, we will expect Gene to be better off than George by about $500. For the player who has enough capital to make bets totaling $1,000,000 over a short period, $500 will not make much of a difference. For the player who takes a long time to make bets totaling $1,000,000, the amount of $500 represents very little when compared with the time spent at the table. Let us also notice that if the bets we mentioned above total $10,000, instead of $1,000,000, then we would expect Gene to be better off than George by about only $5.

Don't pass bettors are often considered "bad luck" at the table (by those players who have bets on the pass line). In gambling jargon, players making don't pass bets are called *don't bettors* or *wrong bettors*. On the basis of the discussion in this section, we observe that if the don't pass bettors are "wrong," then those who make pass line bets are probably "worse."

Many players believe that don't pass bets are the "opposite" of pass line bets. Since the don't pass bettor only ties with an outcome of 12, this is not so.*

In some Casinos, the player ties when 2 (rather than 12) is produced. Since 2 and 12 can each be obtained only in one way, this does not affect the House edge. When the tie takes place with an outcome of 2, the mark

Bar

in the don't pass area of the layout is replaced by

Bar .

Sometimes the tie takes place when 3 is produced. Since 3 can be obtained in two ways, this rule increases the House advantage very substantially. *The edge becomes (surprise!) about 4.1%.*

DON'T COME BETS

As explained above, players are allowed to make don't pass bets only before come-out rolls.

If the next roll is a point roll, and if a player wants to enter the game right away and make a bet similar to a don't pass bet, that player should place a *don't come bet*. Such a bet is made by placing chips in the don't come area (see Fig. 8).

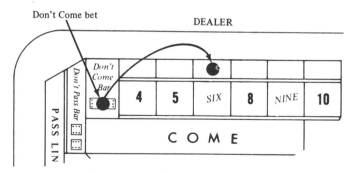

Fig. 8

*The following relation holds: The probability of winning a pass line bet *plus* the probability of winning a don't pass bet *plus* the probability of rolling 12 *equals* 1.

Assume that Carol made a *don't come bet*.

If the outcome of the next roll is 7 or 11, she loses her bet.

If the outcome is 2 or 3, Carol wins *even money*.

If the outcome is 12, she ties.

If the outcome is any other number, say 6, then this number becomes the point* corresponding to Carol's bet. The Dealer moves the bet to the don't come box marked by the number 6 (see Fig. 8).

The bet remains there until either the point or 7 is rolled. If the point is rolled *first*, Carol loses her bet. If 7 is rolled *before* the point, Carol wins even money.

In case of a win, the payoff and the initial bet are moved back in front of the player.

The Casino advantage in the case of don't come bets is the same as in the case of don't pass bets; that is, *about* 1.36%.

The various remarks concerning don't pass bets that were made in the previous section remain valid for don't come bets.

ODDS BETS AND PASS LINE BETS

A player who made a pass line bet may place an additional bet (associated with the pass line bet) called an *odds bet*, as soon as a point is established. The chips representing the odds bet are placed as indicated in Fig. 9.

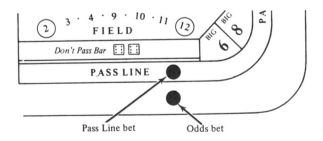

Fig. 9

---

*Usually there are no numbers on don't come boxes. In any case, we shall say, for example, that the boxes behind the point boxes marked by 5 are the *don't come boxes marked by the number 5* (see Fig. 1).

Assume, for example, that George placed a pass line bet before a come-out roll and that the point 6 is established. George may now make an odds bet. The dice will be rolled until *either* 7 *or* 6 is produced. If 7 is thrown *before* 6, George loses the pass line bet and the odds bet. If the point is thrown *before* 7, George wins with both bets.

A pass line bet is always paid *even money* in case of a win. The way the odds bet is paid depends on the point established on the come-out roll. When the point is 6, an odds bet is paid 6 to 5.

The general rules concerning the *payoffs for odds bets* are as follows:

When the point is 4 or 10, the payoff is 2 to 1. Hence, an odds bet of $20 wins $40.

When the point is 5 or 9, the payoff is 3 to 2. Hence, an odds bet of $20 wins $30.

When the point is 6 or 8, the payoff is 6 to 5. Hence, an odds bet of $20 wins $24.

When the player wins, the payoff is made by the Dealer, who places the chips next to the initial odds bet.

In a sense, odds bets decrease the House advantage. In fact, the higher the odds bets are, the smaller the House edge is. (More about this will be said at the end of this section.) In any case, when odds bets equal in amount to the corresponding pass line bets are always taken, *the House advantage (as far as pass line bets with associated odds bets are concerned) is about 0.85%.*

When the Casino allows odds bets twice as large as the corresponding pass line bets and such bets are always taken, *the House advantage (as far as pass line bets with associated odds bets are concerned) is about 0.61%.*

Observe that, percentagewise, a 0.85% advantage is *smaller* than the House advantage in the game of Baccarat or in four-deck Blackjack played under the usual Reno-Tahoe rules or under the *extremely bad* Puerto Rican rules. An advantage of 0.61% is only a little greater than that the House has in the game of four-deck Blackjack when played under the "usual" Las

Vegas strip rules, or in one-deck Blackjack when played under the Reno-Tahoe rules. Regarding Blackjack, we assume that the player uses the corresponding optimal Basic strategy (Zero memory strategy).*

We conclude that *pass line bets with associated odds bets are among the best bets a player can make in a Casino.*

In a large Casino, the lowest value chip found at a Craps table is usually the $1 chip. For this reason, the House cannot pay fractions of a dollar. For instance, if you play at a $5-minimum table, place a $5 odds bet and win with 5 for the point, you should receive $7.50. Since the smallest chips the Casino has are the $1 chips, the player will be paid only $7. In the long run, this increases very substantially the House take. *For this reason, the player should always place only odds bets which can be fully paid. If, for example, the odds bet is $10 or a multiple of $10, the payoff can be made correctly, no matter what the point is.*

The Casino you play in not only might not pay fractions of a dollar, but might not even pay any fraction of the minimum bet allowed at your Craps table.

Since the higher the odds bets are, the smaller the House percent take is, it is important to know the maximum amount allowed for odds bets. This amount depends on the amount of your pass line bet and on the rules in force in the Casino you are in.

The most usual rules are described now.

Single odds. In this case, only odds bets which are *not larger* than the corresponding pass line bets are allowed. For example, if Denny placed a $20 pass line bet, the maximum odds bet he may place is $20.

Double odds. In this case, odds bets which are *twice as large* as the corresponding pass line bets are allowed. For example, if Sheri placed a $50 pass line bet, the maximum odds bet she may place is $100. (As we have seen above, when such bets are allowed, the House edge is only about 0.61%.) Only a few Casinos allow double odds. Even in these Houses. double odds might

---

*See *A Book on Casino Gambling*,¹⁴ Chapter 3.

not be permitted when the corresponding pass line bet is very large.

Full odds. Most Casinos offer full odds. This means that they allow odds bets which might be somewhat larger than the corresponding pass line bets, so that (in case of a win) the payoff may be made correctly. How large the odds bets might be depends on the established point:

When the *point is 4 or 10,* the odds bets cannot be larger than the corresponding pass line bets. We observe that, in this case, a winning odds bet is paid 2 to 1 in case of a win. Hence, it can be paid correctly no matter what its amount is.

When the *point is 5 or 9,* the odds bet may be larger than the corresponding pass line bet, as explained below. Assume that Joan placed a $25 pass line bet and that the minimum value chip at her table is the $1 chip. A $25 odds bet cannot be paid correctly* in case of a win. For this reason, she is allowed to place an odds bet of $26 (26 = 25 + 1). In case of a win, her odds bet pays

$$\$39 \ (39 = 3/2 \times 26).$$

If Joan placed a $15 pass line bet, she is allowed to make an odds bet of $16 (16 = 15 + 1). In case of a win, her odds bet pays

$$\$24 \ (24 = 3/2 \times 16).$$

If Joan placed a $75 pass line bet using $5 chips, she may be allowed to make an $80 odds bet. Hence, she may be allowed to increase the size of her bet not only by $1, but even by one chip of *the same denomination* as the chips used for her initial pass line bet.

When the *point is 6 or 8,* the odds bet can be made as explained below. Assume that Vicki is at a table where the minimum value chip is the $1 chip. She makes a $15, $16 or $17

*When the point is 5 or 9, an odds bet is paid 3 to 2. Obviously, every bet consisting of an even number of chips of the same denomination can be paid correctly. We recall that 2, 4, 6, 8, 10, 12, 14, 16, 18, 20, . . . are the even (strictly positive) integers.

pass line bet. Then the minimum odds bet she is permitted to make is a $15 bet.* If she places an $18, $19 or $20 pass line bet, she is permitted to make a $20 odds bet. Hence, she may increase her bet by, at most $2. If she is at a $1-minimum table and she placed a $1 or $2 pass line bet, she cannot make a corresponding odds bet. If her pass line bet is $3, $4 or $5, she is permitted to make a $5 odds bet. As in the case when the point was 5 or 9, Vicki might be allowed to adjust her odds bet by using chips of the same denomination as those used for her pass line bet.

As a variant to the above rule, if Vicki placed, for example, a $2 pass line bet, she might be allowed to make a $2 odds bet (not a $5 odds bet!). In case of a win, she will be paid only $2 instead of $2.40.

A player who places odds bets associated with pass line bets is said to be *taking the odds*.

Recall that pass line bets cannot be removed on point rolls. Odds bets associated with pass line bets can be removed from the layout before any roll of the dice.

As was said earlier, odds bets decrease the Casino percentage take. In fact, the larger the odds bets are, the smaller this percent take is. Unfortunately, since the player must place additional money on the table when making odds bets, this does not mean necessarily that the total take from the player is less. The following example will clarify these remarks.

Assume that Tom made $10 pass line bets 100 times. The total amount he placed on the table was therefore $1000. The House edge in the case of pass line bets is about 1.41%. It follows that the House is expected to win about 1.41% of $1000; that is, about $14. Now, assume that Tom made odds bets of $10 whenever possible. On the average, two of three come-out rolls will establish a point. Hence, the total amount of money Tom placed on the table is about

$$\$1000 + 2/3 \times \$1000 = \text{about } \$1666.$$

*When the point is 6 or 8, an odds bet is paid 6 to 5. It follows that an odds bet cannot be paid correctly using the minimum value chips found at the table unless such a bet is made in multiples of five such chips.

The House edge is now 0.85%, and 0.85% of $1666 is again about $14. *Hence, the Casino take is the same as before.*

The above remarks show that, *in the long run*, Tom will lose abou the same amount whether or not he makes the $10 odds bets associated with his pass line bets. However, *the player who places $10 pass line bets and takes odds whenever possible is substantially better off than the player who places $20 pass line bets and does not take the odds.*

Similar remarks are valid for the type of odds bets we describe in the following sections.

ODDS BETS AND COME BETS

If Carol made a come bet, she can place an additional bet (associated with her come bet) called, again, an *odds bet*, as soon as a point is established for her come bet.

Assume, for example, that Carol made a come bet on a point roll and that the next roll produces the come point 9. Her bet will be moved to the point box marked by the number 9. Carol may make now an odds bet. She will usually place the chips on the table and will inform the Dealer of her intention (she may say, for instance, "Odds on 9"). The Dealer will place these chips as indicated in Fig. 10. Carol's bets will remain on the layout until *either* 7 *or* 9 is thrown. If 7 is rolled *first*, Carol loses both bets. If 9 is thrown *before* 7, Carol wins with both bets.*

The amount Carol can place as odds bet associated with her come bet depends on the come point. The corresponding rules are the same as in the case of pass line bets.

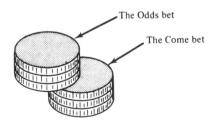

The Odds bet

The Come bet

Fig. 10

*See the remarks in this section concerning *off* and *on* odds bets.

The rules governing the payoffs for odds bets associated with come bets are also the same as in the case of odds bets associated with pass line bets. The payoff is 2 to 1 when the come point is 4 or 10, 3 to 2 when the come point is 5 or 9 and 6 to 5 when the come point is 6 or 8.

In case of a win, the payoff is placed first next to the bets in the point box, and then the total amount is moved to the initial position of the come bet.

An arbitrary rule, which has no justification whatsoever, is the following: An odds bet associated with a come bet is *off* on come-out rolls, unless the player requests the contrary. If the player wants the bet *on* (or *"working"*), a small *on-disc* is placed on the chips. Of course, it would be simpler if these types of bets were always on.

A player who places odds bets associated with come bets is said to be *taking the odds*.

The House advantage in the case of the odds bets described here is obviously the same as in the case of odds bets corresponding to pass line bets. Hence, if odds bets equal in amount to the come bets are taken whenever possible, *and are always on, the House advantage is about 0.85%*. If odds bets twice as large as the corresponding come bets are taken whenever possible, *and are always on, the House advantage is about 0.61%*.

ODDS BETS AND DON'T PASS BETS

A player who made a *don't pass bet* may place an additional bet (associated with the don't pass bet) called, again, an *odds bet*, as soon as a point is established. The chips representing the odds bet are placed as indicated in Fig. 11.

Odds bet (six chips)

Don't Pass bet

Fig. 11

Assume, for example, that John placed a don't pass bet before a come-out roll and that the point 8 is established. John may now make an odds bet. The dice will be rolled until *either* 7 *or* 8 is produced. If 7 is thrown *before* 8, John wins both bets. If the point is thrown *before* 7, John loses both bets.

A don't pass bet is always paid *even money* in case of a win. The way the odds bets associated with don't pass bets are paid depends on the point established on the come-out roll. When the point is 8, an odds bet is paid 5 to 6.

The general rules concerning the *payoffs for odds bets* are as follows:

When the point is 4 or 10, the payoff is 1 to 2. This means that, in case of a win, you will gain an amount equal to *half* of your bet.* Hence, a $60 odds bet brings

$$\$30 \ (= \$60/2).$$

When the point is 5 or 9, the payoff is 2 to 3. This means that, in case of a win, you will gain an amount equal to *two-thirds* of your bet. Hence, a $60 odds bet brings

$$\$40 \ (= 2/3 \times \$60 = 2 \times \$60/3).$$

When the point is 6 or 8, the payoff is 5 to 6. This means that, in case of a win, you will gain an amount equal to *five-sixths* of your bet. Hence, a $60 odds bet brings

$$\$50 \ (= 5/6 \times \$60 = 5 \times \$60/6).$$

When the player wins, the payoff is made by the Dealer, who places the chips next to the initial odds bet.

Odds bets associated with don't pass bets decrease the House advantage. In fact, the higher the odds are, the smaller the House percent take is.

When odds bets equal in amount to the corresponding don't pass bets are always taken, *the House advantage (as far as don't*

*The initial bet is returned to the player (no matter what the point is).

*pass bets with associated odds bets are concerned) is about
0.82%.*

When odds bets twice as large as the corresponding don't pass
bets are allowed and are always taken, *the House advantage (as
far as don't pass bets with associated odds bets are concerned) is
about 0.58%.*

The above percent advantages were computed under the
hypothesis that the odds bets "are paid correctly" in case of a
win. We observe, however, that sometimes it might be impossible for the Casinos to pay fully certain bets. Assume, for example, that you are at a table where the minimum value chip is the
$1 chip, that the point is 8 and that you won a $20 odds bet
associated with a don't pass bet. According to the payoffs rules,
you should receive

$$5 \times \$20/6 = \text{about } \$16.66.$$

Obviously, this is impossible, since the Casino does not have a
66^c chip. In this case, you will be paid only $16. Hence, you lose
66^c. In the long run, such reductions in payoff substantially increase the House take. *Therefore, you should try to place only
odds bets which can be paid correctly. Notice that if your bet is
$6 or a multiple of $6, then it can be paid fully no matter what
the point is, if the table has $1 chips.*

Only a few Casinos allow odds bets twice as large as the corresponding don't pass bets. However, most Casinos permit bets
which, in case of a win, bring the player an amount equal to the
initial don't pass bet. In this case, the odds bet depends on the
point:

When the point is 4 or 10, the player may place an odds bet
twice as large as the initial don't pass bet. Hence, if your don't
pass bet is $35, you will be allowed to place an odds bet of

$$\$70 \ (= 2 \times \$35).$$

When the point is 5 or 9, the player may place an odds bet
equal to 3/2 of the initial don't pass bet. Hence, if your don't
pass bet is $50, you will be allowed to place an odds bet of

$75 (= 3/2 \times \$50 = 3 \times \$50/2).$

When the point is 6 or 8, the player may place an odds bet equal to 6/5 of the initial don't pass bet. Hence, if your don't pass bet is $100, you will be allowed to place an odds bet of

$$\$120 (= 6/5 \times \$100 = 6 \times \$100/5).$$

A player who places odds bets associated with don't pass bets is said to be *laying the odds*.

Although the probability of winning a don't pass bet (under the hypothesis that the roll did not result in a tie) is slightly greater than the probability of winning a pass line bet, most players bet on the line. One of the reasons for this is undoubtedly that the player who lays odds risks more money than the one who takes odds.

ODDS BETS AND DON'T COME BETS

If Robert made a don't come bet, he can place an additional bet (associated with his don't come bet) which is again called an *odds bet*, as soon as a point is established for the don't come bet.

Assume, for example, that Robert made a don't come bet and that the next roll produces the point 5 for Robert's don't come bet. His bet will be moved to the don't come box marked by the number 5.* Robert may now make an odds bet. He will usually place the chips on the table and will inform the Dealer of his intention (he may say, for instance, *Lay odds on* 5 or *Lay on* 5). The Dealer will place these chips near the don't come bet in the same position as in the case of odds bets associated with don't pass bets. Robert's bets will remain on the layout until either 7 or 5 is thrown. If 7 is rolled *first*, Robert wins with both bets. If 5 is thrown *before* 7, Robert loses both bets.

The amount Robert can place as odds bets associated with his don't come bet depends on the point. The rules governing the

*See the footnote on p. 22.

payoffs for odds bets associated with don't come bets are the same as in the case of odds bets associated with don't pass bets.

The type of odds bets described in this section *are always on*.

The Casino advantage, as far as don't come bets and the corresponding odds bets are concerned, is, of course, the same as in the case of odds bets associated with don't pass bets.

A player who places odds bets associated with don't come bets is said to be *laying the odds*.

GENERAL REMARKS

In the previous sections, the main bets a player can place in the game of Craps have been described. Other bets will be discussed in some of the next sections.

The most favorable bets for the player at a Craps table are among those we have already described. They are the following:

Pass line bets
Pass line bets and odds bets
Come bets
Come bets and odds bets
Don't pass bets
Don't pass bets and odds bets
Don't come bets
Don't come bets and odds bets
Place bets on 6 and 8
Pass line bets, odds bets and place bets on 6 and 8

These bets will give the best chance of a winning streak.

While even longer winning streaks (for pass line bettors) have been reported, I would like to say that: 1) In July 1977, at the MGM in Las Vegas, I observed a sequence of twelve successive wins. The probability of such an occurrence is less than 1/4858. 2) In December 1978, at the Desert Inn in Las Vegas, I observed a sequence of ten successive wins. The probability of such an occurrence is less than 1/1180.

Taking and laying odds decreases the Casino advantage. However, when you place odds bets, you risk more money. We suggest that you read again the remarks at the end of the section on odds bets and pass line bets.

When you take or lay odds, you should make only bets which can be paid fully. Otherwise, the House advantage is increased. The amount you have to place on the Craps table might depend on the point.

In Table 3, we give correct amounts of the odds bets corresponding to pass line bets of $5, $13 and $25, respectively.

Table 3.

	$5	$13	$25
Point 4 or 10:	$5	$13	$25
Point 5 or 9:	$6	$14	$26
Point 6 or 8:	$5	$15	$25

For instance, if the player has a $13 pass line bet and the point is 8, a $15 odds bet is allowed.

When the pass line bet is $5 and the point is 5 or 9, Casinos might allow even a $10 odds bet. When the pass line bet is $25 and the point is 5 or 9, the player might make a $30 odds bet.

Certain hedging methods are described later in this chapter.

At a Craps table, the player always bets against the House. If the player wins, the win is paid by the House. If the player loses, the bets are collected by the House.

All the bets described until now, with the exception of pass line bets and come bets, can be removed at any time. All the bets described until now, with the exception of odds bets associated with come bets and place bets, are always *on* (or *working*). The odds bets associated with come bets and place bets are *off* (or *not working*) on come-out rolls, unless the player requests the contrary.

To attract players, certain Casinos offer *coupons* which can be used at the Craps tables. In most cases, the player may place $2 and a coupon as an *even money* bet. In case of a win, the payoff is $3 (the Casino retains the coupon). It is interesting to observe that *the player who places a pass line bet consisting of $2 and a coupon has an advantage of over 23.2%.* Unfortunately, the Casinos will not allow the same person to place many such bets during the same day.

In the game of Craps, the dice are thrown by a player, called the *Shooter*, and not by a Casino employee. When a group of players arrive at an empty table, several dice (usually in a bowl) are placed in front of one of the players. The player will pick two dice and will roll them until a 7 *is thrown on a point roll* (if a 7 is thrown on a come-out roll, the player retains the dice). Then the player loses the dice. The player on the left becomes the Shooter.

The Shooter must place either a pass line bet or a don't pass bet. The Shooter may, of course, place *any* other additional bets.

A player may refuse to throw the dice or may relinquish them at any time. However, players will usually relinquish the dice only after a win or lose decision on pass line bets or don't pass bets.

As we said in the first section of this Chapter, every Craps table has minimum and maximum bets limits. The player should remember, however, that while the maximum amount is allowed for pass line bets, don't pass bets, place bets, etc., it is not necessarily allowed for some of the bets described in the next sections and which offer very high payoffs. The player who intends to bet high should request supplementary information concerning the limits allowed, from the Dealers.

When the Casino personnel do not pay any attention to your questions, remember the procedure recommended at the end of the section on come bets. It always brings the desired results.

BIG 6 AND BIG 8 BETS

A *big 6 bet* is made by placing chips in the area marked *big 6*. A *big 8 bet* is made by placing chips in the area marked *big 8*. Big 6 and big 8 areas are found at two of the corners of the Craps table.

These bets win if the chosen number (6 or 8) is rolled *before* 7 and lose if 7 is rolled *before* the chosen number. In case of a

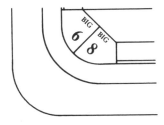

Fig. 12

win, the player is paid *even money*.* Hence, if Zita makes a $50 big 6 bet and the outcome 6 is produced before 7, she wins $50 (so that she collects, in all, her bet included, $100).

The Casino advantage, as far as big 6 and big 8 bets are concerned, is more than 9%.

Recall that place bets on 6 and 8 win and lose the same way as big 6 and big 8 bets. In case of a win, these place bets are paid 7 to 6. The Casino edge corresponding to these bets is about 1.5% (that is, about six times smaller than in the case of big 6 and big 8 bets). In view of the above, one wonders why so many players continue to make big 6 and big 8 bets, instead of the corresponding place bets.

BUY BETS (ALSO CALLED DO COME BUY BETS)

A *buy bet* can be placed on any of the numbers

$$4, 5, 6, 8, 9 \text{ or } 10.$$

To make a *buy bet* on 4, for instance, the chips are placed in one of the point boxes marked by 4. To distinguish such bets from others, a small disc (marked *buy*) is placed on the chips. (Come bets are moved to point boxes as soon as a corresponding point is established, and, as we shall se below, buy bets and come bets are paid differently.)

As in the case of place bets, it is usually the Dealer who places your buy bet in the point box. In case of a win, the payoff and the initial bet are moved back in front of the player.

*This is the usual payoff. However, there are a few places where the payoff for big 6 and big 8 bets is 7 to 6 on wagers of $6 or multiples thereof.

A buy bet can be made or removed at any time. A buy bet is *off* on come-out rolls unless the player requests the contrary (another example of a rule which has no logical justification whatsoever).

A buy bet on 4, for example, remains in the point box, until either 7 or 4 is rolled. If 7 is rolled *first*, the player loses the bet. If 4 is rolled *first* the player wins. The payoff depends on the number you bet on. If the number is 4, as in the above example, the bet is paid 2 to 1.

The general rules concerning *the payoff on buy bets* are as follows:

A buy bet on 4 or 10 is paid 2 to 1.
A buy bet on 5 or 9 is paid 3 to 2.
A buy bet on 6 or 8 is paid 6 to 5.

Notice that the payoff on buy bets is the same as in the case of odds bets associated with pass line bets or come bets.

The buy bets (as well as the lay bets, which we describe in the next section) are not among the most popular ones.

The House advantage in the case of each one of these bets is about 4.8%.

To place a buy bet, the player must *pay a 5% charge* to the House.* For instance, if, at a $5-minimum Craps table, Sandi wants to make a $200 buy bet, she must place $210 on the table: $200 for the bet and $10 for the House (the *charge*). If the bet is removed from the layout, the charge is returned to the player (!?!).

Buy bets should be made in amounts so that the charge can be paid correctly. This is the case, for instance, if *the bets are made in multiples of 20 minimum bets.* If, at a $1-minimum table, you place a $20 buy bet, a charge of $1 is levied. A 5% charge on $10 is $0.50. However, if you place a $10 buy bet, the charge levied is going to be again $1 (this increases substantially the House take).

---

*A 10% charge of $50 is $5. A 10% charge of $20 is $2. A 5% charge is half of a 10% charge. Hence, a 5% charge of $50 is $2.50 and a 5% charge of $20 is $1.

LAY BETS (ALSO CALLED DON'T COME BUY BETS)

A *lay bet* is, in a sense, the opposite of a buy bet. It can be placed on any of the numbers

4, 5, 6, 8, 9 or 10

To make a *lay bet* on 6, for example, the chips are placed in one of the don't come boxes marked by 6. To distinguish such bets from others, a small disc (marked *buy*) is placed on the chips. (Don't come bets are moved to don't come boxes as soon as a corresponding point is established, and don't come bets and lay bets are paid differently.)

As in the case of buy bets, the lay bets are placed by the Dealer in don't come boxes. The player will usually place the chips on the layout (or hand them to the Dealer) and say, for instance, "Lay bet on 6." In case of a win, the payoff and the initial bet are moved back in front of the player.

A lay bet can be removed at any time. The lay bets are always *on*. Remember that buy bets are *off* on come-out rolls.

A lay bet on 6, for instance, remains in the don't come box marked by 6, until *either* 6 *or* 7 is rolled. If 6 is rolled *first*, the player *loses* the bet. If 7 is rolled *first*, the player *wins*.

The general rules concerning the payoff on a lay bet are as follows:

A lay bet on 4 or 10 pays 1 to 2.
A lay bet on 5 or 9 pays 2 to 3.
A lay bet on 6 or 10 pays 5 to 6.

Notice that the payoff on lay bets is the same as in the case of odds bets associated with don't pass or don't come bets. *The average overall House advantage, as far as lay bets are concerned, is about 3.2%.*

To place a lay bet, the player must pay a 5% charge to the House. *However, this charge is levied not on the amount of the bet, but on the amount of the payoff you would receive in case of a win.* For instance, if you place a lay bet of $60 on 5, you would receive $40 in case of a win. The charge you would have to pay is 5% of $40 (not of $60); that is, $2.

The player who decides to make lay bets should be careful and place only bets which can be paid *correctly* and for which the 5% charge can be computed *exactly* (using the minimum value chip found at the table). Otherwise, the House edge will be increased.

HARDWAY BETS

A *hardway bet* is made by placing chips in one of the areas of the table marked by one of the following four pairs:

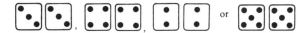

Let us notice that a hardway bet can be removed or made before any roll of the dice.

The outcome (2, 2) is called *hard* 4. The outcomes (1, 3) and (3, 1) are called *easy* 4. The outcome (4, 4) is *hard* 8. The outcomes (2, 6), (3, 5), (5, 3) and (6, 2) are called *easy* 8. In the same way, we define *hard* 6, *hard* 10, *easy* 6 and *easy* 10.

Assume now that Pamela places a *hardway* 8 bet. The bet (if not removed by her) remains on the layout, until *either* 7 *or* 8 is rolled.

If 7 or easy 8 is rolled before hard 8, Pamela loses her bet. Otherwise she wins. Hence, Pamela wins *only* if the outcome (4, 4) is rolled before 7, (2, 6), (3, 5), (5, 3) or (6, 2).

The other hardway bets are settled in a similar way.

A hardway 6 or hardway 8 bet is paid 9 to 1, in case of a win.

A hardway 4 or hardway 10 bet is paid 7 to 1, in case of a win.

The reason for these payoffs is discussed in the next section.

The Casino advantage in the case of hardway 6 or hardway 8 bets is over 9%. The Casino advantage in the case of hardway 4 or hardway 10 bets is over 11%.

The hardway bets are among the best bets for the House.* The relatively high (although improbable) payoffs are one of the reasons why players make such bets. When, on a come-out roll, one of the numbers 4, 6, 8 or 10 becomes the point, many players make hardway bets on that number. For instance, if 10 is rolled on a come-out roll, many players place hardway 10 bets. Of course, there is no justification for this.

It is interesting to observe that if the payoff for hardway 6 and hardway 8 bets were 11 to 1 (instead of 9 to 1), then the player would have a 9% advantage. If the payoff for hardway 4 and hardway 10 bets were 9 to 1 (instead of 7 to 1), then the player would have an 11% advantage. The *fair* payoffs for hardway 6 and 8 bets and for hardway 4 and 10 bets are 10 to 1 and 8 to 1, respectively. With such payoffs, neither the House nor the players would have any advantage.

REMARKS ON THE PAYOFFS OF HARDWAY BETS

On a flight from Las Vegas to the East, a young lawyer, seated on the aisle seat, started to tell me how lucky he had been on this trip to the Mecca of gambling. He said that he had won over $15,000 at the MGM.

I asked if he accomplished this "feat" at the Blackjack tables. After all, it is there that a skillful player has the best chance. Oh no, he said. Most of the Blackjack games he had seen were four-deck games dealt from a shoe and he had "heard" that you cannot win in such games.** *He played Craps!*

When he learned that I wrote on Casino gambling, he explained how puzzled he had been by the fact that the payoffs of the various hardway bets were not exactly the same. Why, he was asking, was the payoff of a hardway 10 bet 7 to 1, and that of a hardway 8 bet 9 to 1. He thought that they should be the same. His "wrong reasoning" was as follows: It is équally likely

---

*When you place a hardway bet and win, you must ask for your initial bet if you want it returned to you. Otherwise, it will be left on the layout and will be considered as a bet for the next roll.
**This is certainly not true. See, for instance, *A Book on Casino Gambling*.[14]

that one would roll (5, 5) or (4, 4). You win (?) the hardway 10 bet if you roll (5, 5) and the hardway 8 bet if you roll (4, 4). Hence, he concluded, the payoffs should be the same.

It was my turn to be puzzled. After all, the answer was quite simple. Of course, it is equally likely for one to roll (5, 5) or (4, 4). However, this does not mean that the considered bets are equally good.

A hardway 10 bet is lost *only* if you roll 7, (4, 6) or (6, 4) *before* (5, 5). A hardway 8 bet is lost *only* if you roll 7, (2, 6), (3, 5), (5, 3) or (6, 2) *before* (4, 4). Hence, you may lose a hardway 10 bet is "three ways" and a hardway 8 bet in "five ways." Therefore, while you win a hardway bet only one way, you will lose hardway 8 bets more often than hardway 10 bets. Hence the payoff of a hardway 8 bet should be higher than that of a hardway 10 bet.

ONE-ROLL BETS

Each one of the bets described below can be placed at any time the player wishes. *Once such a bet is placed on the Craps table, the next roll of the dice decides whether the player wins or loses.*

Field Bets

To make a *field bet*, the player places chips in the *field area*. This area (see Fig. 13) is marked by the numbers

2, 3, 4, 9, 10, 11 and 12.

Fig. 13

The player who made a field bet *wins* if the outcome of the next roll is one of the above numbers and loses otherwise.

In case of a win, the player wins even money if the throw produced 3, 4, 9, 10 or 11. The payoff varies when the outcome is 2 or 12. Most often, a win with such an outcome is paid 2 to 1. *In this case, the Casino advantage is about 5.6%.*

Notice that this percent advantage is about the same as the House edge in the case of *most* Roulette bets. In fact, with the exception of the *five number bet,* * all other Roulette bets give the Casino an advantage of about 5.3% (more precisely, about 5.263157894%!).

After all the field bets are not the worst among those a Craps player can make. Of course, for instance, the pass line bets, the don't pass bets, the place bets on 6 or 8, etc. are better. However, there are many bets which are substantially worse than field bets. For example, the hardway bets, any Craps bets (see below), bets on 7, 11, 2, 12 or 3 (see below), etc.

It is therefore quite amusing to hear a player stating boldly— if not competently—that "field bets are for suckers" and then see this same player making a hardway 8 bet (recall that the House edge as far as this type of bet is concerned is over 9%). This player will even have an explanation ready for this action, if you ask why was the hardway bet made. You will be probably told, with reproach: "Don't you see, the point is 8!!!" Of course, whether or not the point is 8 makes absolutely no difference in the House advantage corresponding to the hardway 8 bet, but our player does not seem to know this yet.

We close this section on field bets by noticing that when, for instance, a win with an outcome of 2 is paid 2 to 1 and a win with an outcome of 12 is paid 3 to 1, *the House advantage decreases to about 2.8%.* However, only rarely does one find a Casino offering such payoffs. When a win with an outcome of 2 or 12 is paid even money, *the House edge is more than 11%.*

---

*At a Roulette table, the *five numbers bet* wins if the outcome is 0, 00, 1, 2 or 3 and loses otherwise. The House advantage corresponding to this bet is about 7.9%. We assume here that the Roulette wheel has "two zeros (0 and 00)" as is the case in most North American Casinos. When the wheel has only "one zero," the House advantage is about 2.7% for all bets (there is no five numbers bet in this case). For more details concerning Roulette, see *A Book on Casino Gambling.* [14]

Any Craps

Any craps are made by placing chips in the middle of the layout, in the area marked

ANY CRAPS.

A player who makes such a bet wins if the outcome of the next roll is 2, 3 or 12 and loses otherwise. The payoff in case of a win is 7 to 1. *The House edge corresponding to this bet is about 11%.*

Any craps bets are discussed further in this chapter in the section about various "hedging" methods.

One-number One-roll Bets

The main *one-number one-roll bets* are those a player can make on any one of the numbers

7, 11, 2, 3 and 12.

These bets are placed in the areas in the center of the layout indicated in Fig. 14. Other *one-number one-roll bets*, or similar type bets, are described in the section following the discussion of craps-eleven bets or horn bets.

For instance, a *bet on* 7 is made by placing chips in the area marked

SEVEN.

If Marty makes such a bet, he wins if the next roll produces 7 and loses otherwise.

We observe that when the shooter rolls 7, every bet on the layout either wins or loses.

A *bet on* 11 is made by placing chips in the area marked

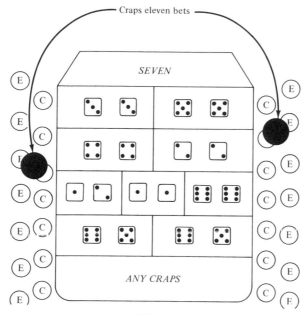

Fig. 14

The player who makes such a bet wins if the outcome of the *next roll* is 11 and loses otherwise. Players often make *bets on* 11 on come-out rolls. In fact, the bet on 11 is the most popular one-number one-roll bet.

The usual payoffs for the one-number one-roll bets are the following:

A bet on 7 is paid 4 to 1, in case of a win.
A bet on 11 is paid 14 to 1, in case of a win.
A bet on 2 is paid 29 to 1, in case of a win.
A bet on 12 is paid 29 to 1, in case of a win.
A bet on 3 is paid 14 to 1, in case of a win.

The House advantage in the case of each one of the bets mentioned above is over 16%.

We notice that, *percentagewise,* the one-number one-roll bets are the worst for the player.

Some generous Casinos increase some of the payoffs indicated above. In this case, a somewhat different type of center layout is sometimes displayed (see Fig. 15). This type of layout is encountered mostly in the Reno-Tahoe area.

For bets on 2 and 12, the payoff might be increased to 30 to 1. In this case, *the House advantage is reduced to about 14%.*

For bets on 3 and 11, the payoff might be increased to 15 to 1. In this case, *the House advantage is reduced to about 11%.*

For the reader's information, it should be noted that the fair payoffs for bets on 2 and 12 and for bets on 3 and 11 are 35 to 1 and 17 to 1, respectively.

Craps-eleven Bets (or Horn Bets)

Craps-eleven bets (or horn bets) are made by placing the chips as indicated in Fig. 14. On certain layouts, there is a special box for this type of bet (see Fig. 15).

The player who places a craps-eleven bet wins if the outcome of the next bet is 2, 3, 11 or 12 and loses otherwise. The exact payoff depends on the number produced, and on the Casino you are in. For example, in most Casinos on the Las Vegas strip, the player is paid 6.75 to 1 if 2 or 12 is produced and 2.75 to 1 if 3 or 11 is rolled. In this case, *the House advantage is about 15%.* In other Casinos, especially in the Reno-Tahoe area, a

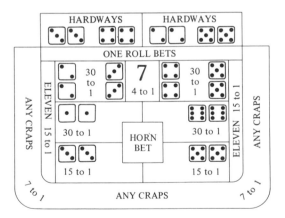

Fig. 15

craps-eleven bet is paid 6.75 to 1 if 2 or 12 is produced and 3 to 1 if 3 or 11 is rolled. In this case, *the House advantage is 12.5%.*

We observe that a craps-eleven bet cannot be paid correctly using minimum table chips, unless they are made in multiples of four such chips.

For example, on the Las Vegas strip, a $4 horn bet is paid $27 if the outcome is 2 or 12 and $11 if the outcome is 3 or 11. In the Reno-Tahoe area, a horn bet is paid, again, $27 if the outcome is 2 or 12 and $12 if the outcome is 3 or 11. Hence, at a $1-minimum table, a $4 horn bet can be paid correctly, using $1 chips, in both cases.

Other One-roll Bets

In certain Casinos, the player is allowed to make one-roll bets on any "possible" outcome. For instance, on 5 or 8 or an easy 8, etc. The payoffs vary from Casino to Casino.

Somewhat more common are the one-roll bets the player can make on any one of the pairs

$$(2, 2), (3, 3), (4, 4) \text{ or } (5, 5).$$

On certain layouts you may find special areas where such bets can be placed (see Fig. 15). These one-roll bets should not be confused with the hardway bets described in a previous section. For example, the player who makes a one-roll bet on (3, 3) wins if the outcome of the next roll is (3, 3) and loses otherwise.

When the payoff for bets on any one of the outcomes

$$(2, 2), (3, 3), (4, 4) \text{ or } (5, 5)$$

is 30 to 1 (see Fig. 15), *the corresponding House advantage is about 14%.*

A FEW REMARKS CONCERNING HIGH PAYOFF BETS

When you place a $10 pass line bet on the table, you are paid even money in case of a win. When you place a $10 bet on 12, you will be paid $290 in case of a win.

Remember also that the House advantage in the case of pass line bets is substantially smaller than that in the case of bets on 12. In fact, it is about eleven times smaller.

Certain players argue that "one cannot win big" by placing only pass line bets. Their argument is based on the fact that the payoff for pass line bets is 1 to 1. We shall briefly examine this argument.

The *probability** that a player wins a pass line bet is

$$976/1980 = \text{(somewhat more than) } 0.49292.$$

The *probability* that a player wins with a bet on 12 is

$$1/36 = \text{(about) } 0.02778.$$

If you bet $10 on 12, you have a probability equal to 0.02778 to win $290.

Now let us assume that you start by placing a $10 bet on the pass line. If you win, you bet $20 (= 2 times $20) on the pass line, and so on. *If you win five times in a row, you will make $310.*

The probability that you will win five times in a row can be easily computed.** It is somewhat greater than***

$$0.02909.$$

Surprise! The chance of winning five pass line bets in a row is greater than that of winning a bet on 12. Moreover, if you bet on the line in the manner indicated above and win, you will gain $20 more than if you bet on 12.

---

*Remember that the *probability of an event* measures its likelihood of occurrence. The larger the probability, the greater the chance of occurrence of the corresponding event.

**If p is the probability of winning a pass line bet, then the probability that you will win such a bet five times in a row is

$$p^5 = p \times p \times p \times p \times p.$$

***We notice that 0.02778 is about 1/36 and 0.02909 is about 1/34.37.

HEDGING PASS LINE BETS AND DON'T PASS BETS

Sometimes players "hedge bets," especially large ones. These players make second bets* which, so they think, compensate completely, or at least in part, for the main bet. They believe that, by proceeding this way, the House advantage is cancelled or reduced substantially. Unfortunately, this is not true. The results of such methods are, in a sense, just the opposite. The House edge is increased when compared to that corresponding to the best bet involved in the hedge.

In any case, since some of the hedging methods are quite popular, we shall describe a few here.

Assume that John made a $100 pass line bet before a come-out roll. Since this is a large bet for his bankroll, he is afraid that he might lose it on the come-out roll. To "insure" against such an eventuality, he places a $15 any craps bet. If 2, 3 or 12 are rolled on the first throw, he loses the $100 pass line bet, but wins

$$\$105 \ = \ 7 \ \times \ \$15$$

with his second bet. Hence, he has a net profit of $5.

At first his method might seem good. But is it really so? The answer is *no!* Notice that if the shooter produces 7, 11 or a point, the $15 is lost. This decreases the return on the $100 bet, when John wins his main bet. In the long run, the House edge will be increased.

In fact, it is hard to understand why John wants to hedge his pass line bet on the come-out roll, since on this roll he already has the advantage. He would do better to worry about what will happen on the point rolls. Only then the House "starts" to have the edge.

But maybe John does not know or does not believe that he has the edge on the come-out roll. After all, many players and even authors of books on gambling do not know this elementary fact. In a book copyrighted in 1972, the author, who is intro-

---

*Sometimes more than one additional bet is made.

duced as a "professional gambler" (what is that?) repeatedly makes the *ridiculous* assertion that on the come-out roll a Natural (that is, 7 or 11) is rolled as often as Craps (2, 3 or 12). I must apologize to the reader for interrupting our discussion of hedging methods with these remarks, but I find such a statement concerning Naturals and Craps quite unbelievable. Even the chance of rolling 7 is substantially greater than that of rolling 2, 3 or 12.

Returning now to the hedging method, observe that, to make certain he will not lose on the come-out roll, it is enough for John to place an any craps bet equal to *one-seventh* of his pass line bet. However, one-seventh of $100 is about $14.28571. Of course, for practical reasons, no one can make such a bet. This is why John made a $15 any craps bet.

In any case, if whenever you place a pass line bet, you also place an any craps bet equal to one-seventh of the pass line bet, then as far as these bets are concerned, *the House has an advantage of about 1.65%.*

If the any craps bets are larger than one-seventh of the corresponding pass line bets, the House advantage is increased.

When we compare the 1.65% edge obtained above with that of 1.41% in the case of pass line bets, we see that the hedging method described here has as its effect an increase in the Casino advantage.

A similar method of hedging is used sometimes in the case of come bets.

Players who make don't pass bets or don't come bets hedge by betting on 7 and 11. The results of such methods are similar to those indicated above.

Some players simultaneously make pass line and don't pass bets of equal amounts. When a point is established, they take odds.* These players believe that they play even with the House. Once they "play even," they are convinced that "with a little bit of luck" they will end big winners.

---

*We assume that these odds bets are equal in amount to the initial bet.

These players reason as follows: The pass line and don't pass bets "cancel" each other and hence the only significant bets on the layout are the *fair* odds bets. It is true that the odds bets have fair payoffs, but in the *Casino game*, the pass line and don't pass bets *do not* cancel each other. If (6, 6) is thrown on the come-out roll, half of the amount on the table is lost.

In fact, in the case when bets are placed as indicated here, *the House edge is about 1.04%*.

This advantage is calculated with respect to the amount placed on the table.

We conclude that the House percent take corresponding to pass line or don't pass bets, with associated odds bets, is smaller than that in the case of the hedge discussed here.

Sometimes players start by placing a pass line bet. When a point is established, they take odds and make a don't come bet. When a point is established for the don't come bet, odds are layed. I shall not discuss this hedge in detail. Observe, however, that if a 7 is thrown on the roll following the come-out roll, *all* the bets on the layout are lost. The final conclusion concerning this hedge is similar to those for the hedges discussed before.

Notice again that some of the bets involved in the hedges described here are better than the hedges themselves! Also, some of these hedging methods are awkward. For these reasons, these hedges will not be listed among the best bets in the game of Craps (in the final section of this chapter), although some of them give the House a very low edge (not as low, however, as some of the bets used to build the hedge).

After reading the above remarks, some readers might wonder why so many players play such hedges. Consider the popular hedge described first. As we have seen, the player who uses this hedge will lose more per dollar, in the long run, than the player who simply makes pass line bets. However, this player will win *more often* than the player who bets on the pass line, although the amounts won are smaller than those won by the player who bets on the line. Simple calculations (which are not presented here) show that the probability that the player who uses the first hedge will win is about

$$0.60404.$$

Compare this with the probability of winning a pass line bet, which is about

$$0.49292.$$

Similar remarks are valid for the other hedges described in this section.

CHEATING IN DICE GAMES

Cheating in dice games is encountered much more often than is generally assumed. It is done mainly in the following two ways:

1. By introducing into the game dice which favor certain combinations. These are so-called *crooked dice.*
2. By controlling the throw; that is, throwing the die or dice in such a way that certain combinations favoring the cheater occur more often. For instance, when participating in a Craps game and making pass line bets, the cheater will try to roll 7 or 11 on the come-out roll.

It is possible to roll the dice so that certain outcomes are produced more often than they are normally. This is easier to accomplish if you are not required to throw the dice far from you and make them bounce off a backboard. In any case, players who can perform such feats are very rare. Most cheaters use crooked dice.

Crooked dice can be manufactured in many ways. In a sense, we can divide most of them into three categories. One category consists of dice with modified shapes. Another category consists of dice into which weights have been introduced close to one or more of their faces. The last category consists of dice which are not marked as they should be. For example, one or more numbers may be marked twice on the same die. Since you cannot see more than three of the faces of a die from the same position, such dice are not easy to detect.

Fig. 16

Of course, crooked dice, no matter what type they are, are used for the same purpose; namely, to influence the outcome of the throw.

Below we shall describe in more detail some of the dice in the three categories mentioned above. Several indications as to what advantage the cheater has when using crooked dice are given at the end of this section.

Assume that the faces of a die marked by 6 and 1* are "shaved down" (see Fig. 16). Thus, these two faces remain the same size as before, but the size of each of the other four is somewhat decreased. It is obvious that *when we roll this die, the faces which have greater area will come to rest on the table more often than those having less area.* Hence, the die described here will favor the outcomes 1 and 6. Such a die is often called a *6-1 flat* (or a *six-ace flat*).

Note that *when you roll a pair of 6-1 flats, the outcomes 7, 2 and 12 are favored.*

The 5-2 flats and the 4-3 flats are produced in the same manner. *When, for example, you roll a pair of dice consisting of a 6-1 flat and a 4-3 flat, the favored outcomes are 10, 9, 5 and 4.*

One could also "shave down" the two faces marked, respectively, by 6 and 3. The die so modified will favor the outcomes 6, 4, 3 and 1. *A pair of such dice will produce a 7 somewhat more often than is normal.*

Still another method of modifying the sizes of the faces of a die consists in cutting some edges more than others or cutting them at different angles.

---

*Remember that most dice are marked so that the sum of numbers on *opposite faces* is 7.

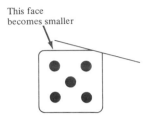

The "modification" of the die in this Figure is exaggerated

Fig. 17

If one or more of the faces of a die are rounded (see the die on the left in Fig. 18), the die will rest less often than normal on one of the rounded sides. Hence, the numbers on the faces opposite to the rounded ones will occur less often than expected. If the die is modified as indicated in Fig. 18 (see the die on the right side), then the face indicated by the arrow will rest more often than normal on the playing surface. Hence, the number on the opposite face will occur more often than expected.

The dice in the second category are the so called *loaded dice*. When additional weights* are inserted close to one or more of the faces of a die, these faces will tend to rest on the playing surface more often than normal when the die is rolled.* Hence, the numbers on the opposite faces will be favored.

Loaded dice might be, and usually are, perfect cubes. It is only the added weights which make them favor certain outcomes.

For example, if you insert weights close to the face marked by 6, the number 1 will occur more often than is normal.

Dice are usually loaded in the following manner: All "the dots" on the die are drilled "a little deeper." The holes, except, for example, those on the face marked by 4, are filled with black paint. The remaining four holes are also filled with black paint but a little heavy metal (for instance, lead or platinum) is inserted as well. The die is now loaded. The outcome 3 will be favored by this die. If "the work" is good, the extra weights

---

*The additional weights move the "center of gravity" of the die closer to the chosen faces.

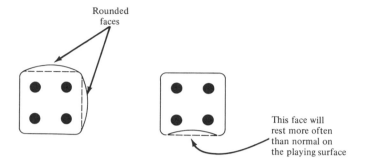

Rounded
faces

This face will
rest more often
than normal on
the playing surface

The "modifications" of the dice in this Figure are exaggerated

Fig. 18

cannot be detected by eye inspection, even when the die is transparent.

The best way of checking a die suspected of being loaded is to immerse it in a glass of water. Note the face pointing upwards when the die comes to rest at the bottom of the glass. Repeat the experiment a few times. If the upper face is the same most of the time, the die is probably loaded.

One other type of crooked die we describe here is the *hollowed die* (also called *floater*). If, for example, a die is hollowed under the face marked by 6, the effect is the same as if weights were inserted close to the face marked by 1. Such a die will favor the outcome 6. Hollowed dice are generally opaque.

Dice on which one or more numbers are marked twice are called, in gambling jargon, *misspots* or *tops* or *tops and bottoms*.

For example, consider a die on which each one of the numbers 5, 4 and 1 is marked twice. On actual crooked dice, the marking is done so that the same number appears on opposite faces. A pair of such dice will never produce, for example, 7 or 12. It can produce only one of these numbers:

$$2, 5, 6, 8, 9 \text{ and } 10.$$

In the game of Craps, such a pair of dice will favor the pass line bettors.

We want to observe that dice belonging to one of the first two categories described above do not always produce the desired outcomes. However, they produce these outcomes more often than is normal. For instance, if you roll a 6-1 flat, you might produce 2, 3, 4 or 5. However, you will produce 6 and 1 more often than is normal and 2, 3, 4 or 5 less often than is normal. Observe that you cannot make crooked dice behave normally, *no matter how you throw them!* A 6-1 flat, for instance, will produce 6 and 1 more often than is normal whether or not you make the die bounce off a backboard.

Crooked dice belonging to one of the first two categories described will *give the cheat an advantage in the long run (if the dice are adequately chosen).* The dice in the third category described above are different. Certain outcomes cannot be produced, no matter what! For instance, a pair of misspots such as those described above in the text, will never produce 6 or 7. Two 6-1 flats may produce 6, for example, but they will produce 6 less often than is normal and 2, 12 and 7 more often than is normal.

Naive persons might think that misspots are never really used. It would be too brazen! Certainly, one may assume that posh Casinos will not use such dice. Unfortunately, in private games, etc., this is not necessarily so. Consider a player who is stupid enough to enter into a game with two or three apes he barely knows. Assume that some other player introduces misspots into the game. Our naive player sees something suspicious and asks to check the dice. The cheater and some of the apes protest, with indignation. "What! You do not trust us?" What will our friend do in such a situation? If the incident occurs as described above, it is almost certain that the player who introduced the misspots works with the apes. If our naive player is a "believer in his rights" and insists on checking the dice, he will probably lose more than the money in his pocket.

Another method, not described above, of making a die favor certain outcomes consists of placing on certain of its faces a special glue-like substance. This will cause the faces so prepared to rest more often than is normal on the playing surface, when the die is rolled. For instance, if you place a substance on the face marked by 6, the die will favor the outcome 1. This method of cheating has an additional advantage. It is very hard to prove anything, since, if the substance is good, it will last on the die only a very short time. This kind of "crooked die" is usually called a *honey die* or *honey*.

Another type of crooked dice are the *magnetic dice*. These dice are controlled by magnets placed under the playing surface.

Of course, there are other methods which should also be considered *cheating*. For example, deliberate mishandling of the rules of the game, with the purpose of obtaining an advantage, is obviously cheating. An example of this kind of cheating is described at the end of the section on come bets. In that example, the Dealer, a young man, moved the player's bet to the "previous point." By doing this, he substantially increased the House advantage. Recently, I observed the same "method" used in several Casinos in Reno. Players, therefore, should always be careful and follow the games closely, no matter where they play. Underpaying certain players and/or "forgetting" to pay certain bets is also cheating.

Do many players cheat, or at least try to cheat, in dice games? The answer to this question is, unequivocally, yes! Most of the cheaters introduce crooked dice into the game by "sleight of hand." For example, consider the game of Craps. The cheater starts by hiding the crooked dice, say in the right hand. The cheater picks up the honest dice from the table, with the same hand, and releases the crooked ones. When done expertly, the move cannot be detected. Brazen cheaters, or players cheating for the joint where the game takes place, might even use both hands for such "operations."

An easy way of introducing crooked dice in a Casino game of Craps is to replace the dice bouncing off the table onto the floor by crooked ones. It is true that one of the Boxmen inspects the dice which fall on the floor before using them again, but this is definitely not enough. Only when the dice have certain special markings known only to the Boxmen can the Casino achieve *a certain degree of safeguard* against cheaters. The usual Casino emblems are not enough for identification. In a Craps game, the pair of dice the shooter uses is chosen from several dice in a bowl. A group of cheaters working together could easily replace all or most of the dice at the table in a relatively short time. Once the change has taken place, the cheaters will have the advantage in the long run (if the "right kind" of crooked dice were introduced into the game).

The above remarks concern cheating done by players. But what about the joints offering various dice games? More particularly, what about legal Casinos? Are they all honest? Considering the situation in Blackjack, one cannot infer that there is no cheating in any of the dice games offered in these places. In any case, one should observe that most of the cheating in Blackjack is done by sleight of hand, while the use of crooked dice is material evidence in case of inspection.

On the basis of the information we have, we conclude that, in large Casinos, the dice games are honest.

We end this section with a few examples in which we discuss the advantage the cheater has when using various types of crooked dice. Observe that choosing the right kind of crooked dice for obtaining a desired result is, in a sense, a real "art."

Remember that the most usual payoff for a bet on 2 is 29 to 1, in case of a win. Remember also that, as far as this bet is concerned, the House has an advantage of over 16%.

Now assume that crooked dice favoring the outcome 2 are introduced into the game! For example, a pair of dice hollowed under the faces marked by 6 will favor the outcome 2. The probability of throwing 2 has now been increased. Assume that this probability is increased by only

$$1/50 = 0.02.$$

Calculations show that the House advantage no longer has the edge, as far as the bet on 2 is concerned. *The player now has an advantage of over 41%.*

Assume that in a game of Craps a cheater making pass line bets introduces a pair of misspots on which each one of the numbers 1, 4 and 5 is marked twice. This pair of dice can produce only the numbers

2, 5, 6, 8, 9 and 10.

Since 7 cannot be produced, the player will win each time a point is established. The only way the cheater can lose is when 2 is produced on the come-out roll. Since on each of the dice 1 is marked twice, it follows that there are four ways of producing 2. Hence, the cheater will lose with probability 4/36 and win with probability 32/36. It follows that *the cheater has an advantage of over 77%, as far as pass line bets are concerned.* Compare this with the 1.41% advantage the House has when the game is played with honest dice.

Assume that 6-1 flats are introduced into a game of Craps. When such dice are used, the outcome 7 will be obtained more often than is normal. It follows immediately that the House advantage is increased, in relation to the players making place bets. How large the House edge is depends on how great is "the bias" of the dice used in the game. In fact, in this case,* the more the dice are biased, the greater the House advantage is.

Assume again that a pair of 6-1 flats are introduced into a Craps game. It is generally believed that in this case the House advantage over the pass line bettors is increased and that the don't pass bettors gain an edge over the House. I made a complete study of 6-1 flats with the help of Henry Cejtin and Robert Welland, who did a series of computer calculations. The fact is that the beliefs mentioned above are correct only within certain limitations. The House edge over the pass line bettors increases when 6-1 flats, which are not extremely biased, are introduced into the game. The House advantage increases with "the bias"

*Observe that this is not necessarily true in all cases (see below).

of the dice and attains a maximum when the probabilities of 1
and 6 are close to 2.15/6 (instead of 1/6). Once the bias is
beyond this, the House edge starts to decrease. When the dice
are "extremely biased," the House loses almost *all* the advantage over the pass line bettors. When the probabilities of occurrence of 1 and 6 are close to 2.15/6, the House edge is about
21%.

Under the same conditions, the don't pass bettors have an advantage of about 18.5% over the House.* When the dice are
"extremely biased," the House again has the advantage, and
this time the edge is substantially more than when the game is
played with honest dice.

PROBABILITIES AND FAIR PAYOFFS IN CRAPS

*The contents of this section are not necessary for the reading
and understanding of this chapter.* In any case, the player might
want to know the probabilities of winning certain bets in the
game of Craps, and the corresponding fair payoffs. This is why
this section is inserted here. In relation to these remarks, it
should be noted that I have already indicated what are the best
bets in the Casino game of Craps (these indications will be
presented again in the next section) and that in these games the
payoffs are fixed by the House. However, the information given
below is very important in the private game of Craps (which is
described in a section in Chapter 2). In such games, the players
often make bets among themselves and decide what the payoffs
should be. The players who have better knowledge of the fair
payoffs of various bets will have the advantage.

Table 4 has two columns. In the first column we list the **Bets**
and in the second the corresponding **Probabilities of Winning**.

More precisely, the probability of winning a pass line bet is

976/1980.

*A number of years ago, a friend of mine spent several days in Las Vegas playing
Craps. One day when he returned to his "favorite Casino," he found it closed, for
cheating at dice. Since most of the players make pass line bets, cheating joints will
generally use dice favoring the outcomes 6 and 1. My friend was making only don't pass
bets and hence he might have been favored by such crooked dice.

Table 4.

Bet	Probability of Winning
Pass line bet	About 0.49292
Don't pass bet	About 0.47929
Come bet	About 0.49292
Don't come bet	About 0.47929
Craps-eleven bet	1/6
Field bet	4/9

The probability of winning a don't pass bet is

949/1980.

Table 5 has three columns. In the first we list the **Bets** and in the second the corresponding **Probabilities of Winning**. In the third we list the **Fair Payoffs**. Remarks concerning fair payoffs follow the table.

An 8 to 1 payoff for a certain type of bet means that if you make such a bet and win, you will receive *eight times* the

Table 5.

Bet	Probability of Winning	Fair Payoff
Place bet on 4	3/9	2 to 1
Place bet on 10	3/9	2 to 1
Place bet on 5	4/10	3 to 2
Place bet on 9	4/10	3 to 2
Place bet on 6	5/11	6 to 5
Place bet on 8	5/11	6 to 5
Hardway 4 bet	1/9	8 to 1
Hardway 10 bet	1/9	8 to 1
Hardway 6 bet	1/11	10 to 1
Hardway 8 bet	1/11	10 to 1
Any Craps	1/9	8 to 1
Bet on 7	1/6	5 to 1
Bet on 11	1/18	17 to 1
Bet on 2	1/36	35 to 1
Bet on 3	1/18	17 to 1
Bet on 12	1/36	35 to 1

amount you placed on the table. Your initial bet is returned to you.

A 3 to 2 payoff is the same as a 3/2 to 1 payoff; a 6 to 5 payoff is the same as a 6/5 to 1 payoff.

A payoff of a bet is *fair* when neither side participating in the game has any advantage.

Once we know the probability of winning a bet, the corresponding fair payoff (to the bettor) can be easily calculated. A "formula" which can be used to compute such payoffs is given at the end of this section.

When you make a bet which has a payoff higher than the fair payoff, you will have the edge. When you make a bet which has a payoff lower than the fair payoff, you are at a disadvantage.

Observe that, in the Casino game of Craps, none of the bets listed in Table 4 have fair payoffs.

To decrease the size of the remaining tables, they will be set up somewhat differently than the above ones.

The following notation will be used: For any two outcomes a and b, we denote $P(a, b)$ the probability that a occurs before b.

For instance, $P(4, 8)$ is the probability that 4 is rolled before 8. Of course, $P(8, 4)$ is the probability that 8 is rolled before 4.

In the following tables we list various probabilities of the form $P(a, b)$ and the "corresponding fair payoffs." The payoff listed "to the right" of $P(a, b)$ is the fair payoff to the player who bets that a will be produced before b, and wins.

It follows from Table 6 that, *in the Casino game of Craps, the payoffs of all types of odds bets are fair.*

We conclude this section with the following remarks. Assume that John made a *certain bet*. Assume that the probability of winning is p and that of losing q. Then:

(*) *the fair payoff to John is q/p to 1*

If, for example, John placed a bet on 7,

$$p = 1/6 = 6/36 \text{ and } q = 30/36.$$

Table 6.

Probability	Fair Payoff	Probability	Fair Payoff
$P(4, 7) = 3/9$	2 to 1	$P(7, 4) = 6/9$	1 to 2
$P(10, 7) = 3/9$	2 to 1	$P(7, 10) = 6/9$	1 to 2
$P(5, 7) = 4/10$	3 to 2	$P(7, 5) = 6/10$	2 to 3
$P(9, 7) = 4/10$	3 to 2	$P(7, 9) = 6/10$	2 to 3
$P(6, 7) = 5/11$	6 to 5	$P(7, 6) = 6/11$	5 to 6
$P(8, 7) = 5/11$	6 to 5	$P(7, 8) = 6/11$	5 to 6

Table 7.

Probability	Fair Payoff	Probability	Fair Payoff
$P(4, 5) = 3/7$	4 to 3	$P(5, 4) = 4/7$	3 to 4
$P(4, 6) = 3/8$	5 to 3	$P(5, 6) = 4/9$	5 to 4
$P(4, 8) = 3/8$	5 to 3	$P(5, 8) = 4/9$	5 to 4
$P(4, 9) = 3/7$	4 to 3	$P(5, 9) = 1/2$	1 to 1
$P(4, 10) = 1/2$	1 to 1	$P(5, 10) = 4/7$	3 to 4

Table 8.

Probability	Fair Payoff	Probability	Fair Payoff
$P(6, 4) = 5/8$	3 to 5	$P(8, 4) = 5/8$	3 to 5
$P(6, 5) = 5/9$	4 to 5	$P(8, 5) = 5/9$	4 to 5
$P(6, 8) = 1/2$	1 to 1	$P(8, 6) = 1/2$	1 to 1
$P(6, 9) = 5/9$	4 to 5	$P(8, 9) = 5/9$	4 to 5
$P(6, 10) = 5/8$	3 to 5	$P(8, 10) = 5/8$	3 to 5

Table 9.

Probability	Fair Payoff	Probability	Fair Payoff
$P(9, 4) = 4/7$	3 to 4	$P(10, 4) = 1/2$	1 to 1
$P(9, 5) = 1/2$	1 to 1	$P(10, 5) = 3/7$	4 to 3
$P(9, 6) = 4/9$	5 to 4	$P(10, 6) = 3/8$	5 to 3
$P(9, 8) = 4/9$	5 to 4	$P(10, 8) = 3/8$	5 to 3
$P(9, 10) = 4/7$	3 to 4	$P(10, 9) = 3/7$	4 to 3

Since

$$q/p = 30/6 = 5,$$

it follows that the corresponding fair payoff is 5 to 1. Observe that this is the payoff listed in Table 5. Also observe that, in the Casino game of Craps, the corresponding payoff is only 4 to 1. Since this is lower than the fair payoff, the player is at a disadvantage.

Formula (*) shows that the fair payoffs for pass line bets and for don't pass bets are

$$\text{about } 1.02868 \text{ to } 1$$

and

$$\text{about } 1.02845 \text{ to } 1,$$

respectively. Obviously, such payoffs are not possible in actual games. One cannot pay $0.02868 or $0.02845. In any case, note that the usual 1 to 1 payoff is lower than the payoffs indicated above. This is why the House has the edge in the case of pass line bets and don't pass bets.

THE BEST BETS IN THE GAME OF CRAPS

In the previous sections were described the bets a player can make in the game of Craps. Among them, the *best bets* are the following:

PASS LINE BETS
PASS LINE BETS AND ODDS BETS
COME BETS
COME BETS AND ODDS BETS
DON'T PASS BETS
DON'T PASS AND ODDS BETS
DON'T COME BETS
DON'T COME BETS AND ODDS BETS
PLACE BETS ON 6 AND 8
PASS LINE BETS, ODDS BETS AND PLACE BETS ON 6 AND 8

Odds bets should be taken and laid, *no matter what the point is.*

It is substantially better to place $10 pass line bets and take odds whenever possible, than to place $20 pass line bets.

Place only odds bets which can be paid *correctly.* Otherwise, the House advantage will be increased. (One should remember, however, that whether or not the player may make such bets can sometimes depend on the amount of the initial pass line or don't pass line bet.)

For the same reason, the player should make only place bets which can be paid *correctly.*

Remember that odds bets associated with come bets are *off* (*are not working*) on come-out rolls, unless the player requests the contrary. If the player wants the bets *on* (or *working*), a small *disc* or one of the *point markers* is placed on the chips.

2. Other Games with Dice

Among the criteria used when deciding what dice games to describe in this chapter were the following:

1. Interesting structure
2. Popularity
3. Historical interest
4. Interest for the player or for the House

To shorten and unify this Chapter, we present most of the games as played between a player and the House. *The House may be a Casino, another player or any opponent. The player may be a group of players.*

When a player makes a bet, a win is paid according to specified rules. In case of a loss, the bet is collected by the House.

It is obvious that sophisticated players will want to know if they have an advantage or a disadvantage in the games they play. These players will find, in practically all cases, the needed information in this chapter. No reasonable player will risk much money in a highly disadvantageous game. In private games, the player should try, if possible, to assume the role of the House, when the House has the advantage.

Among the games described here, special attention is paid to the *Private game of Craps*. This is, of course, due to the popularity of this game. The reader will see that, when played under the usual rules, the *Shooter* is at a disadvantage. Hence, when you play in a private game, you should decline to roll the dice, if possible. Various bets which give a nice profit in the

Private game of Craps are described in detail in the corresponding section.

To clarify further some of the ideas presented above, let us assume that you and Jill decide to play *the first game of the Chevalier de Méré.** If you have a choice, you should play the role of the player and let Jill play that of the House. *Why?* Obviously, because as indicated in the text in *the first game* the player has the advantage. If you play the part of the player, you will win when at least one 6 is obtained in four rolls of a die. When a 6 is not obtained, Jill will win. When you win, Jill will pay you. When she wins, she will take your bet. Of course, unless you trust Jill completely, all money or chips necessary for paying a win or a loss should be placed "on the table." In fact, even if you trust your opponent, it is better if all bets are placed on the table at the beginning of the game. It is much easier to be paid from money on the table than it is to settle later, if ever. If you and Jill decide to play *the second game of the Chevalier de Méré,* then for the same reasons as above you should play the part of the House and let Jill play that of the player.

Of course, the above recommendations are based on the assumption that you want to win. However, if you are a gentleman and if Jill is beautiful you might want to let her win. In this case, you and she should change sides.

When you play a game in a Casino, the advantage, in the long run, will be on the side of the House. "Luck," whatever that is, cannot overcome, *in the long run*, an edge against you. Those who believe in "luck" might want to wonder why all the Casinos are "so lucky" and most players "so unlucky."

In any case, there is one exception to what I have said above. It is furnished by the game of 21 or Blackjack, when played under reasonable conditions.** Unfortunately, the game is played only rarely under such conditions! The player who wants to play Blackjack should try to find a four-deck game in which the *Joker* (or *plastic card*) is not inserted very high. The player

---

*See the description of this game and that of *the second game* in this Chapter.
**This implies, of course, "reasonable rules." If you are not allowed to double on any two cards, etc., the rules should be considered *bad*.

should also make certain (this is very, very hard) that the cards were well shuffled before they were placed in the shoe. In this case, a *highly skillful* player can obtain an advantage over the Casinos. You should not believe, however, that you will become skillful by studying the game the night before leaving for Atlantic City or Las Vegas. *Do not play* in games dealt from a five-deck or six-deck shoe. *It is ridiculous to patronize these games.* Most players who sit in on such games might as well hang around their neck a plate with the inscription:

SUPER SUCKER.

I strongly recommend to these players that they play Craps instead of Blackjack. Also, the non-expert should not play in games in which the deck or decks are kept in hand.

Returning to the material in this chapter, observe that all the games presented here are described completely, clearly and in detail. Since the description of some of the games (for instance, that of the game General) requires many details, it may take a certain memorization effort to master them. It is, however, better to have a complete description than one which on the surface looks relatively shorter but *does not make sense*, and which nobody (including the person who wrote it) understands.

With the exception of Backgammon, which should be also considered a dice game, all the other important games are discussed here. Unfortunately, it is impossible to write something useful about Backgammon in a limited space. A full-length book would be necessary for discussing this game.

Some of the dice games described in this chapter can be played, in certain Casinos, using electronic machines. For example, certain versions of *Chuck-a-luck* or *High dice* can be played in this manner.

I close this introduction by indicating that this Chapter also contains several *new games* (for example, *One-die Craps, High dice Craps,* etc.) never described before. Some of them would make very attractive Casino games.

THE PRIVATE GAME OF CRAPS

The Private game of Craps can be played by any group of persons who have the time, two dice and the money necessary for bets.

The players gather around a horizontal and relatively smooth surface on which the dice will be rolled. It is preferable that the dice are thrown against a backboard or a wall (see Fig. 1).

The rules under which the game is played are similar to those used in Casinos. They might depend on the knowledge of the game the players have.

An enterprising person, having enough capital, may suggest that the game be played under the *usual Casino* rules and may "offer" to play the role of the House. If the other players accept this suggestion, *our enterprising friend will make a nice profit.*

However, *the Private game of Craps is played, usually, in the following manner:* One of the players, for instance, John, is chosen* to be the *starting Shooter*. If he accepts to roll the dice,

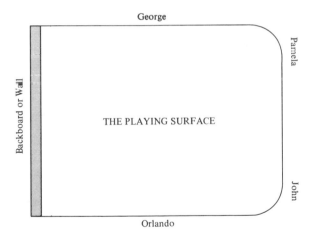

Fig. 1

*The players may, for instance, each roll a die. The one who throws the highest number is the designated Shooter. Ties can be settled by repeated throws. If the designated Shooter refuses to roll the dice, the player on the left becomes the Shooter.

he will *first* place a certain amount, say $60, on the playing surface. The other players may agree to *cover** this amount. For instance, George, Pamela and Orlando may place on the playing surface $25, $10 and $25, respectively. These bets by John and by the other players are usually called *center bets*.

Observe that, in the above example, the total amount of the center bets placed by George, Pamela and Orlando *equals* John's center bet. Below we shall see what happens when this is not the case.

John will now start to roll the dice. If he throws 7 or 11 on his *first roll*, he wins. If he throws 2, 3 or 12 on the *first roll*, he loses. If the outcome of the *first roll* is any other number (that is, 4, 5, 6, 8, 9 or 10), then this number becomes the *point*. John will continue to roll the dice until he produces either the point or 7. If the point is rolled *before* 7, John wins. Otherwise he loses.

In case of a win, John collects the bets placed by George, Pamela and Orlando. When John loses, George, Pamela and Orlando win $25, $10 and $25, respectively.

We observe that, *as far as his $60 center bet is concerned, John is in the same situation as the player who places a $60 pass line bet in a Casino Craps game.* Hence, in the long run, he will lose about 1.41% of the total amount of his center bet. *The players who cover John's bet have a 1.41% advantage.*

The Shooter loses the dice when a 7 is thrown on a point roll. The player on the left becomes the new Shooter (observe that this player might not want to roll the dice). The Shooter may relinquish the dice at any time, after a win or lose decision.

In private games, skillful players often refuse to become Shooters. Why? Because when the game is played as indicated above, the Shooter is at a disadvantage. Recall that in Casino games it makes no difference who throws the dice.

What happens when John accepts to be the Shooter and his $60 center bet is not covered fully? In most games, John has the option to either withdraw part of his bet or to refuse to throw the dice. If John refuses to roll the dice, the player on his left becomes the Shooter. When the center bet placed by the other

*In old gambling jargon, the term *fade* was sometimes used.

players totals more than $60, John may either increase his center bet, or refuse some of the bets made against him.

To avoid discussions, the players should adopt some rule as to how their center bets can be placed. For example, the player to the left of the Shooter could be the first allowed to place a center bet. If this player does not cover completely the Shooter's bet, the next player to the left may be the one allowed to place a center bet, etc.

Once the Shooter is ready to start rolling the dice, various bets, different from the initial center bets, can be placed between the players (including the Shooter) gathered around the playing surface. Many bets are often placed as soon as a point is established.

For example, assume that the point is 4. Pamela may offer to pay 3 to 2 to anyone who bets that John will roll the point before 7. If George accepts her offer and places such a $10 bet, he will win $15 if 4 is rolled before 7 and will lose otherwise.

Observe that the probability to roll 4 before 7 is

$$P(4, 7) = 3/9.$$

Hence, for "the game between Pamela and George" to be *fair*, she should offer a 2 to 1 payoff. With a 3 to 2 payoff, *Pamela has an edge of over 16%.*

These remarks might give us an idea as to what "a private friendly game" may mean for an unskillful player. The Private game of Craps is a gold mine for the player who has a good knowledge of the probabilities and fair payoffs* of the various possible bets, and who can find enough "suckers" to play the game.

When the game is *honest* and is played as indicated in this section, *you will always have an advantage when you cover center bets placed by the Shooter.* Your edge will be about 1.41%. In private games, do not accept to roll the dice.

Of course, the players might decide to play the game under rules somewhat different from those described here. In this case, some of our conclusions might have to be modified.

Observe that the variety of bets encountered in private games is greater than that in Casino games. And remember that you should never make bets whose fair payoffs you do not know.

Tables of bets and corresponding fair payoffs can be found in Chapter 1. The player should not try to learn these tables by heart. In any case, before you place a bet you are not familiar with, you should check its fair payoff.

This section concludes with descriptions of two more bets. You will make a nice profit if you find somebody willing to accept them. These bets are as follows:

Assume that John offers to pay 2 to 1 to anyone betting that the Shooter will produce *at least one* 7 in the next two rolls and that Marty accepts (?) the offer! The probability of obtaining at least one 7 in two rolls is 11/36. The probability that Marty loses is 25/36. From the formula (*), Chapter 1, we deduce that the fair payoff to Marty is

$$25 \text{ to } 11, \text{ that is, about } 2.27 \text{ to } 1.$$

Since John pays only 2 to 1, he has a very nice edge. In fact, John's advantage is about 8.3%. If, during a playing session, Marty covers $100 bets 20 times, he is expected to lose about $166.

If Marty does not like the first offer, John might "change the bait" and try again. He may offer to pay 2 to 1 to anyone betting that the Shooter will produce *either* 6 *or* 7 in the next roll. It is interesting to notice that the probability that this occurs is again 11/36. We conclude that the bet is advantageous to John and that his edge is the same as before; that is, about 8.3%.

BAHAMA CRAPS

Bahama Craps is a variant of the game of Craps which was described in detail in Chapter 1. Basically, it is the same game. However, when you play Bahama Craps, you cannot make *come bets, don't come bets* and *place bets*.

In a sense, the Bahama Craps rules slow down the game

---

*A list of such probabilities and payoffs are given in Chapter 1.

somewhat. The players who place mainly pass line, come, don't pass and don't come bets will have to wait for a come-out roll (remember that in the section on pass line bets, in Chapter 1, I indicated that it takes about 3.37 rolls of the dice to settle a pass line bet). The players who want to enter the game right away will be forced to make less favorable bets; for instance, buy bets.

Bahama Craps is played in the Bahama Islands, England, etc. The game is also known under the name *New York Craps*.

The layout used in Bahama Craps corresponds, of course, to the bets offered in the game. Hence, it is somewhat different from that shown in Fig. 1, Chapter 1. Also, the Casino employees are positioned around the table differently than, for instance, in Nevada or Atlantic City.

THE TWO-DICE HAZARD

As was said in the historical note in Chapter 1, the old game of *Two-dice Hazard* (which shall be called here *Hazard*) is generally considered to be the ancestor of modern Craps. Due to its *historical interest, it is described here in detail.* To facilitate the

Playing Hazard

Fig. 2

understanding of the rules, modern terms are used. Here we discuss the game of Hazard as played between two players, whom we shall call Robert and John. We assume that Robert is the *Shooter* and that he pays John's wins and collects his losses.

The game proceeds as follows: John places a bet and Robert rolls a pair of dice until the outcome is one of these numbers:

5, 6, 7, 8 or 9.

This outcome becomes *John's point* (or the *player's point*).

The pair is now rolled once more. When the *outcome* of this roll is the same as John's point, or one of the numbers 2, 3, 12 or 11, the game ends right away, according to the *following rules:*

1. The outcome is John's point: John loses.
2. The outcome is 2 or 3: John wins.
3. The outcome is 12: John wins if his point is 5, 9 or 7 and loses if his point is 6 or 8.
4. The outcome is 11: John wins if his point is 5, 6, 8 or 9 and loses if his point is 7.
5. When the outcome is neither John's point nor one of the numbers 2, 3, 12 or 11, it must be

4, 5, 6, 7, 8, 9 or 10

   and it must be different from John's point. In this case, the outcome becomes the *Shooter's point.* Now the dice continue to be rolled *until* either the player's point or the Shooter's point is produced. If the player's point is rolled *first*, John wins. If the Shooter's point is rolled *first*, John loses.*

The Shooter used to be called the *Caster*, the player's point the *Main* and the Shooter's point the *Chance*.

---

*It is obvious that Hazard and Craps are related. It is also obvious that of the two, the game of Craps is the simpler and the more elegant one.

When Hazard is played according to the above rules:

The probability that John wins is about 0.50917
The probability that Robert wins is about 0.49082.

We conclude that if the payoff to the player is 1 to 1, *John has an edge of about 1.83%.**

Hence, the Shooter is at a disadvantage. To make the game more even, de Montmort suggested in his book[21] that the rule concerning a throw of 12 (which was presented above) be modified as follows: John wins if his point is 5 or 9 and loses if his point is 6, 8 or 7. It is interesting to recall that, in the usual game of Private Craps, the Shooter is also at a disadvantage.

Of course, more than one player may participate in the game. In fact, there can be as many as can stand around the table (assuming that the game is played on a table). Any player who entered the game when John did wins when John wins and loses when John loses.

In the usual version of the game, the Shooter could refuse certain bets made against him. When the game was played in some establishments, a cut was taken from the Shooter's wins, according to certain rules. The players (including the Shooter) could usually make additional bets among themselves. Of course, among the players who made such bets, those who had more knowledge had an advantage. The dice were generally released by the Shooter after a losing decision.

On the basis of the remarks in this section, we see that there was no advantage whatsoever in being the Shooter.

In his book,[21] de Montmort also discusses a *Three-dice game* which has a structure basically similar to that of Two-dice Hazard.

It might be interesting to notice that Charles Cotton con-

---

*We assume that John's bet is not removed before the final win or lose decision is reached. When the outcomes 2, 3, 4, 10, 11 and 12, on the first roll, are considered ties, John's advantage is only 1.22%.

cludes the section on Hazard in his book by saying that happy is he who decides not to play Hazard anymore, and that even more happy is he who never heard the name of the game!

ONE-DIE CRAPS

The game is played with *one die* on a table with a layout as that in Fig. 3. It is conducted by a Stickman and one or two Dealers. The Stickman and the Dealers represent the House. The number of players participating in the game is limited only by the space available around the layout.

The players may place three kinds of bets: *pass line bets, odds bets associated with pass line bets and one-number one-roll bets*.

The House pays the wins of the players and collects their losses.

As in the game of Craps, there are two types of throws in One-die Craps: *come-out rolls* and *point rolls*.

Every roll following a throw having 1 for an outcome is a come-out roll. The game starts with a come-out roll. The *point marker* is placed clear of point boxes when the roll is a come-out. When the *point marker* is "inside" one of the point boxes (see Fig. 3), the throw is a point roll.

We shall now examine in detail the bets mentioned above.

Pass Line Bets

The disc labeled *A* in Fig. 3 represents a *pass line bet*. Such bets are allowed only before come-out rolls.

Assume that John made a pass line bet before a come-out roll. If the outcome of the roll is 1, he wins *even money*. If the outcome is 2 or 3, he *loses* his bet. If the outcome is any other number (that is, 4, 5 or 6) then this number becomes the *point*. In this case, the *point marker* is moved to the corresponding box. For instance, if the outcome of the come-out roll is 5, the point marker will be placed in the point box marked by the

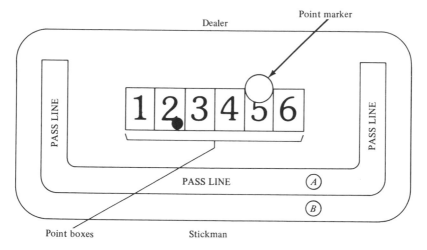

Fig. 3

number 5. The die continues to be rolled (these throws are called *point rolls*) until the outcome is *either* 1 *or* the point.

If 1 is rolled *before* the point, John loses his bet. If the point is rolled *before* 1, John wins. When the point is 4 or 5, the player is paid *even money* in case of a win. When the point is 6, the player is paid 2 to 1.

When the outcome of a point roll is either 1 or the point, the next throw is a come-out.

Odds Bets

A player who made a pass line bet is allowed to place an additional bet, called an *odds bet*, once a point has been established. The disc labeled *B* in Fig. 3 represents such a bet.

Assume that John made a pass line bet before a come-out roll and that the outcome of the roll is 5. John may now make an odds bet. The die continues to be rolled until the outcome is *either* 1 *or* 5. If 1 is rolled *before* 5, John loses the pass line bet and the odds bet. If 5 is rolled *before* 1, John wins with both bets. As seen above, the payoff for the pass line bet depends on the point. The odds bet is always paid 2 to 1, in case of a win.

The amounts allowed for odds bets depend on the corresponding pass line bet and on the rules imposed by the House.

One-number One-roll Bets

The player can place *one-number one-roll bets* on any one of these numbers:

$$1, 2, 3, 4, 5 \text{ or } 6.$$

The black disc in Fig. 3 represents such a bet on 2. If George made this bet, he wins if the next throw produces 2 and loses otherwise. The other one-number one-roll bets are settled in the same way. The payoff is 4 to 1, in case of a win.

The House advantage in the case of pass line bets is about 8%. When odds bets equal in amount to the corresponding pass line bets are taken whenever possible, *the House advantage decreases to about 5.5%.* We observe that this edge is about the same as that in the case of most Roulette bets (see p. 41). When odds bets twice as large as the corresponding pass line bets are made, *the House advantage is about 4%.* In the case of one-number one-roll bets, *the House advantage is about 16%.*

A bet similar to the don't pass bet in the usual game of Craps can be easily introduced into One-die Craps. However, such a bet does not give any advantage to either side and this is why it is not considered in this game.

It should be observed that, in the game described here, the die is rolled by one of the players (the *Shooter*). The die passes from one player to another according to rules similar to those adopted in the usual game of Craps.

NOSAL'S SIMPLIFIED CRAPS

An interesting game played with two dice was invented by Miloslav Nosal.* Here we describe the game as played between a player and the House.

*See Nosal's *Basic Probability and Applications,*[22] p. 175.

To participate in the game, the player makes a bet and the dice are rolled. The player wins if the outcome is one of the numbers

$$2, 3, 4, 10, 11 \text{ or } 12$$

and loses otherwise. Hence, the player loses when the outcome is one of these numbers:

$$5, 6, 7, 8 \text{ or } 9.$$

In case of a win, the payoff depends on the number produced:

If the outcome is 2, the player is paid 3 to 1.
If the outcome is 3 or 4, the player is paid 1 to 1.
If the outcome is 10 or 11, the player is paid 2 to 1.
If the outcome is 12, the player is paid 5 to 1.

In this game, *the House has an advantage of about 2.8%.*

BARBOTTE

Barbotte is a simplified version of Craps. It is played mostly in Canada. The player makes a bet, and two dice are rolled until one of the pairs

$$(3, 3), (5, 5), (6, 6), (6, 5), (5, 6)$$

or

$$(1, 1), (2, 2), (4, 4), (1, 2), (2, 1)$$

is obtained.

If a pair in the first sequence is produced first, the player wins *even money.* If a pair in the second sequence is produced first, the player loses the bet.

Since there are six ways of obtaining a pair in the first sequence and also six ways of obtaining a pair in the second sequence, Barbotte is a *fair* game.

When the game is played in some establishments, a cut is taken from each win.

Barbotte is also known as *Barbudi* or *Barbooth*.

DOUBLE THE SIXES

Here we describe the game as played between two players, Jill and Jack.

One die is rolled *four times*. The number of times 6 is produced is counted. We denote this number by A.

If, for example, the four rolls produced 1, 2, 6 and 5, then A = 1. If the rolls produced 6, 1, 1 and 6, then $A = 2$.

The same die is now rolled *eight times*. The number of times 6 is produced is counted. We denote this number by B.

If, for example, the eight rolls produce 1, 2, 1, 6, 6, 1, 2 and 5, then $B = 2$. If the rolls produce 1, 1, 2, 6, 6, 6 and 4, then B = 3.

The win or lose decision depends on the values of A and B.

When $A = 0$, Jack wins if B is 2 or greater and ties otherwise.

When $A = 1$, Jack wins if B is 2 or greater and loses otherwise.

When $A = 2$, Jack wins if B is 4 or greater and loses otherwise.

When $A = 3$, Jack wins if B is 6 or greater and loses otherwise.

When $A = 4$, Jack wins if B is 8 and loses otherwise.

Hence, when A is different from zero, Jack wins when B is equal to $2A$ or greater and loses otherwise. When A is zero, Jack cannot lose.

When Jack wins, he receives $1 from Jill. When Jack loses, he pays $1 to Jill. In case of a tie, neither player gains or loses anything. *Who has the advantage in this game, Jill or Jack?*

To many players it seems "obvious" that there is at least an even chance that the number of sixes obtained in eight rolls is double that obtained in four rolls. Recall also that Jack cannot lose when A is zero.

A recent survey has shown that a large majority believes that

Jack has the edge. *Since this is not so, we must conclude that this game is very deceptive.*

Calculations, which are not presented here, show that in the dice game of Double the sixes, *Jill has the advantage. Her edge is about 1.5%.*

Hence, while Jill's advantage is not huge, it is in any case somewhat greater than that of the House in the case of pass line bets in the game of Craps. It should be observed that the above conclusions are not affected if, instead of rolling four times one die, we roll once four dice, and instead of rolling eight times one die, we roll twice four dice.

How Did the Game of Double the Sixes Originate?

The idea at the basis of the dice game Double the sixes originated in a question posed by Samuel Pepys* to Sir Isaac Newton** (1642–1727).

Samuel Pepys asked Isaac Newton the following:

Denis throws a die *six times* and wants to produce *at least one six*. Carol throws a die *twelve times* and wants to produce at least *two sixes*. Marina throws a die *eighteen times* and wants to produce at least *three sixes. Decide whether or not Carol and Marina have at least as good a chance to succeed as Denis has.*

Newton solved the problem and showed that *Denis has a better chance to succeed than Carol and Carol has a better chance to succeed than Marina.* If we denote by *p, q* and *r* the respective probabilities of success of Denis, Carol and Marina, the above conclusion is expressed by the relations

$$p > q > r.$$

From the correspondence between Newton and Pepys, it

*Samuel Pepys was a Britisher who had an industrious, adventurous and worthwhile life. In a certain sense, he was also quite successful. He was one of the Presidents of the Royal Society and was a Secretary to the Admiralty. He kept a secret diary, which was published in 1825, many years after his death. The intrigue stories, sex stories, etc. make fascinating reading and throw much light on human nature.
**Galileo Galilei and Isaac Newton contributed immensely to the development of Science.

seems that the latter was not very happy with the answer. It is true that the result might appear surprising. Nevertheless, Newton's solution is correct. Note that Pepys asked his question is 1693. Not very many mathematicians would have been able to solve the problem then. Since then we have "progressed," and today every university student who has taken a mathematics course should be able to find the solution to Pepys' problem.

HIGH-LOW

When it is offered in Casinos, a layout like that shown in Fig. 4 is sometimes used.

The player may place bets in the area marked *low* or in that marked *high*. The win or lose decisions are made on the basis of the outcome of a roll of *two dice*.

The player who placed a bet on *low* wins *even money* if the outcome of the roll is one of the numbers 2, 3, 4, 5 or 6 and loses otherwise.

The player who placed a bet on *high* wins *even money* if the outcome of the roll is one of the numbers 8, 9, 10, 11 or 12 and loses otherwise.

There are 15 ways of producing 2, 3, 4, 5 or 6. Hence, a bet on *low* can be won in 15 ways and lost in 21 ways. The same is true for a bet on *high*. Notice that the House collects all bets on the layout when the outcome is 7.

Sometimes the player is allowed to make a bet on 7. In this case, the player wins if the outcome of the roll is 7 and loses otherwise. A bet on 7 is paid 4 to 1, in case of a win. Observe

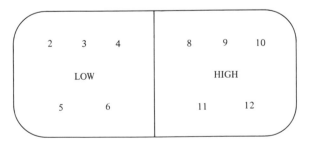

Fig. 4

that the payoff is the same as that for a bet on 7 in the game of Craps.

The House edge in the case of each one of the three bets mentioned above is exactly the same. It is over 16%.

The game described here is also known under various other names; for example, as *Seven* or *Manque-Passe*. The English words corresponding, in this context, to *manque* and *passe* are *fails* and *passes*, respectively.

MATCHING DICE

The game is played with a pair of dice. The player makes a bet and the dice are rolled. The player wins if the outcome of the roll is one of the pairs

$$(1, 1), (2, 2), (3, 3), (4, 4), (5, 5) \text{ or } (6, 6)$$

and loses otherwise.

When the player is paid 4 to 1 in case of a win, *the House has a 16% advantage*.

When the player is paid 5 to 1 in case of a win, the game is *fair. Neither side has any advantage*.

When the player is paid 6 to 1 in case of a win, *the player has a 16% advantage*.

The chance of rolling a pair different from the six listed above appears to many even greater than it really is. Therefore, a gambler should not have too much difficulty finding an opponent willing to offer a 6 to 1, or even greater, payoff. In such a case, our gambler will win quickly and substantially.

A similar game can be played with a coin. Imagine, for example, that Carol and Tom each throw a coin. Carol wins if both throw the same side. If they throw different sides (for instance, if Carol throws heads and Tom throws tails), then Tom wins. When playing this way, Carol and Tom have the same probability of winning. Hence, if Tom pays Carol $1 when she wins and collects $1 from her when she loses, the game is fair.

To verify the above assertions, take note that there are *two* ways of throwing the same side and *two* ways of throwing different sides. If one were to find "a coin having three sides" (this would be quite a trick!), the same type of game would give Tom a substantial advantage.

HIGH DICE

This game can be played with any number of dice.

To participate in the game, the player makes a bet. The dice are rolled and the numbers produced on each one of them are added. The total is the *House point*. The same dice are rolled again. The total obtained this time is the *player's point*.

The player wins if the player's point is higher than that of the House, and loses otherwise.

In case of a win, the player receives even money.

When the game is played with *one die*, the House advantage is about 17%. When the game is played with *two dice*, the House advantage is about 11%. When the game is played with *three dice*, the House advantage is about 9%.

Note that ties are taken by the House. If the ties were ignored, the game would be fair. The reader who wants to verify this assertion should imagine that the House point is established using *white dice* and that the player's point is obtained using *red dice*. It is obvious that the chance of rolling a higher total with the white dice is the same as that of rolling a higher total with the red dice.

The game described above is also known as *High point*.

HIGH DICE CRAPS

This game is an interesting version of High dice. It is played with two dice. We shall describe it here as played between a player, Robert, and the House.

To participate in the game, Robert makes a bet. The two dice are then rolled until a number equal to 4 or greater is produced. Hence, the dice are rolled until the outcome is one of these numbers:

4, 5, 6, 7, 8, 9, 10, 11 or 12.

If the outcome is 11 or 12, the player wins *even money*. If the outcome is one of the numbers

$$4, 5, 6, 7, 8, 9 \text{ or } 10,$$

then this number becomes *the point*.

The pair of dice is now rolled once more. If the outcome is *higher* than the point, Robert wins *even money*. Otherwise he loses his bet.

For example, assume that the first two rolls produced 3 and the third roll produced 8. If the outcome of the fourth roll is any of the numbers

$$9, 10, 11 \text{ or } 12,$$

Robert *wins*. If the outcome is any of the numbers

$$2, 3, 4, 5, 6, 7 \text{ or } 8,$$

Robert *loses* his bet.

In this game, the House has an advantage of about 2.35%.*
The bets described above are obviously similar to the pass line bets in the game of Craps.

THE CHEVALIER DE MÉRÉ'S DICE GAMES

The First Game

To participate in the game, the player makes a bet. A die is rolled four times. The player wins *even money* if 6 is produced *at least once*. Otherwise the House** wins.

*We assume that the bets made in the game remain on the table until the final win or lose decision is reached.
**Remember that *House* may mean any opponent; for instance, an opposing player. Who rolls the die makes, of course, no difference. The player wins if 6 is produced *at least once*. For example, assume that the outcome of the first throw is 5 and that of the second 6. In this case, the player has won. There is no need to roll the die two more times. Similar remarks are valid for the second game.

In this game, *the player has an advantage of about 3.5%*.

If the win or lose decision is taken by rolling the die only three times, then the House has the advantage.

The Second Game

To participate in the game, the player makes a bet. A pair of dice is rolled 24 times. The player wins *even money* if (6, 6) is produced *at least once*. Otherwise the House wins.

In this game, *the House has an advantage of about 1.7%*.

If the win or lose decision is taken by rolling the pair of dice 25 times, then the player has the advantage.

It is obvious that the more you throw the pair of dice, the better is the chance of obtaining (6, 6). It follows that the House will have the advantage if you roll the dice 24 or fewer times. The player has the edge if you roll the dice 25 or more times.

The Legend of the Chevalier de Méré

The *legend* says that the Chevalier de Méré was a devoted gambler. He used to bet even money on making at least a 6 in four throws of a die. He was making so much money that after a while nobody wanted to play this game against him. He offered then to bet even money on making at least a (6, 6) in 24 rolls of a pair of dice. To his surprise, he was now losing. He then consulted Blaise Pascal (1623–1662, French philosopher, mathematician, scientist and man of letters), who explained why the player loses in the second game.

Whether or not the Chevalier de Méré was a devoted gambler is not absolutely certain. In any case, the questions he asked led to a certain progress in probability theory, a Science which nowadays has many and varied applications in so many fields.

While the Chevalier did not determine the exact number of throws which would assure the player's advantage in the second game, he came close to it. A recent survey shows that a majority believes that, for the second game to be favorable to the player, it is enough to throw the dice more than 18 times. This is presumably due to the fact that the probability of the outcome (6, 6) is 1/36 and 36/2 = 18. As we know, this is highly inaccurate.

FIVE ROLLS OF A DIE

Jill makes a bet and rolls a die *five times.*

If she rolls *an even number three or more times,** she wins. Otherwise she loses.

In case of a win, Jill is paid 3 to 2 by Jack. If she loses, Jack collects her bet.

If, for example, Jill bet $20 and rolled

$$2, 6, 5, 4, 4,$$

she will win $30. In fact, in this case *Jill rolled four even numbers.*

Since the chance of rolling an even number is the *same* as that of rolling an odd number, many players believe that the game is even. A recent survey of a number of college students confirms this statement. However, this is not the case. *In fact, in this game, Jill has the advantage. Her edge is huge. It is 25%.* Recall that this means that *in the long run* Jill will win an amount equal to about a quarter of the sum of all bets she makes.

Calculations show that the probability that Jill produces three or more even numbers in five rolls is 1/2. Hence, her probability of winning is the same as that of losing. The huge advantage Jill has is due to the 3 to 2 payoff she receives in case of a win. *The fair payoff for this game is 1 to 1.*

A similar game can be played with a coin.

TWENTY-SIX

Twenty-six was very popular in many taverns, especially in the North American Midwest. It is still played in many places. The role of the House is usually assumed by a bartender or by the owner of the establishment.

To participate in the game, the player chooses one of the numbers

$$1, 2, 3, 4, 5 \text{ or } 6$$

*Among the numbers 1, 2, 3, 4, 5 and 6, the even numbers are 2, 4, 6 and the odd numbers 1, 3, 5.

as *point* and places a bet. *Thirteen dice are thrown (usually from a cup) ten times!** The total number of times the point is produced is counted. The player *wins* if this number is *at least* 26 and loses otherwise.

The payoff is as follows: If the number of times the point is produced is 26 or more but less than 33,** the player is paid 3 to 1. If the point is produced 33 or more times, the payoff is 7 to 1.

When played under the above rules, *the House edge is about 24%*.

Note that the payoffs mentioned above are not adopted universally. They are, however, the most common ones. Sometimes a payoff is offered when the number of times the point is produced is 11 or less or when it is exactly 13.

If the 3 to 1 and 7 to 1 payoffs would be replaced by 4 to 1 and (about) 18 to 1, respectively, Twenty-six would become a *fair* game. Under such conditions, neither the player nor the House would have any advantage.

When played in taverns, the House cannot make very much money with this game. It is true that the House edge is huge, but the bets are quite small most of the time. However, since once the game is started it takes a fairly long time to finish it (even without the usual interruptions), the establishment will sell at least a few more Martinis.

THE COIN-DIE GAME

Ralph and Jackie play the following game: A *coin* is tossed and a *die* is rolled. If the outcome of the coin toss is *head*, Ralph pays Jackie a number of dollars equal to twice the number rolled with the die. If the outcome is *tail*, Jackie pays Ralph $4 *plus* a number of dollars equal to the number rolled with the die.

For example, if *head* is tossed with the coin and 5 is rolled

---

*This is equivalent to rolling 10 dice 13 times or rolling one die 130 times.
**This means that the point was produced 26, 27, 28, 29, 30, 31 or 32 times. The probability of this event is less than 1/5, but greater than 1/6. The probability that the point is obtained at least 33 times is less than 6/1000.

with the die, Ralph pays Jackie $10. If *tail* is tossed with the coin and 3 is rolled with the die, Ralph receives from Jackie

$$\$4 + \$3 = 7.$$

Who has the advantage in this game, Ralph or Jackie? Calculations show that Ralph has the advantage. *In the long run, he will have a gain of about $0.25 per game.*

If Ralph receives from Jackie $5 (instead of $4) plus a number of dollars equal to the number rolled with the die, then he will make about $0.75 per game.

ROLLS OF THREE DICE

When we roll *three dice*,

$$216 = 6 \times 6 \times 6$$

different outcomes are possible. (Although it is not difficult to prove this assertion, I do not want to burden the reader with such details.)

In any case, to facilitate the understanding of the discussion below, assume that our *three dice* have different colors. One is *white*, one is *green*, and the remaining one is *red*.

If we roll the dice and if, for example, 3 is rolled with the *white* die, 5 with the *green* die and 6 with the *red* one, we say that we *rolled* (or *threw*) (3, 5, 6) or that the *outcome* is (3, 5, 6).*

We have already noted that 216 different outcomes are possible. As in the case of one or two dice, these 216 outcomes are *equally likely*. Hence, when we roll three honest dice on a table, we have no reason to expect that we have more of a chance to

---

*The *object* (3, 5, 6) is a *triple*. Here are several other examples of triples: (1, 2, 3), (money, yacht, blonde), etc. Two triples (*u, v, w*) and (*a, b, c*) are equal if and only if *a* = *u*, *b* = *v* and *c* = *w*. The *order* in which the elements of a triple are written is essential.

roll (3, 5, 6) than, for instance, (6, 6, 2). The probability of rolling, say, (1, 6, 1), is 1/216.

If we threw, for example, (3, 5, 6), the corresponding *sum* or *total* would be 14 (= 3 + 5 + 6). Of course, the total is again 14 whenever we roll (5, 3, 6), (4, 5, 5), (6, 6, 2), etc. It can be shown that the total 14 can be obtained in 15 different ways.

If we throw (3, 5, 6) and if we are interested only in the corresponding sum, we shall say that we *rolled* (or *threw*) 14 or that the *outcome* is 14.

Table 1 shows in how many ways the various possible *totals* can be obtained.

When we roll three dice, the outcomes having the least chance of occurrence are 3 and 18. The outcomes having the best chance of occurrence are 10 and 11.

It might be interesting to observe that the results in Table 1 seem to have appeared in print for the first time in a publication of Galileo Galilei (1564–1642).

We say that we rolled *three of a kind* when we produce the same number with each one of the dice. There are six different three of a kind outcomes; namely,

(1, 1, 1), (2, 2, 2), (3, 3, 3), (4, 4, 4), (5, 5, 5), (6, 6, 6).

The probability of rolling *three of a kind* is

$$\frac{6}{216} = \frac{1}{36} .$$

We close this section with a few remarks.

Table 1.

3 and 18 can (each) be rolled only in 1 way.
4 and 17 can (each) be rolled in 3 ways.
5 and 16 can (each) be rolled in 6 ways.
6 and 15 can (each) be rolled in 10 ways.
7 and 14 can (each) be rolled in 15 ways.
8 and 13 can (each) be rolled in 21 ways.
9 and 12 can (each) be rolled in 25 ways.
10 and 11 can (each) be rolled in 27 ways.

Assume that Denis and Jill play the following game: One of them rolls three dice. If the outcome is 10, Denis *receives* $1 from Jill. When the outcome is 9, Denis *pays* Jill $1. *In this game, Denis has an advantage of about 0.9%.* *

For the readers interested in knowing how such conclusions are reached, we present, without many explanations, the corresponding calculations (for more details, see the section on expectation in Chapter 3): The probability that Denis wins $1 is 27/216. The probability that he loses $1 is 25/216. Hence, his *expected gain* per $1 is

$$1 \times \tfrac{27}{216} - 1 \times \tfrac{25}{216} + 0 \times \tfrac{164}{216} = \tfrac{2}{216} \,.$$

We conclude that his *percent advantage* is

$$100 \times (2/216) = \text{(about) } 0.92592 = \text{(about) } 0.9.$$

GOING TO BOSTON

The game is played with three dice. To describe it, we must understand first what is *the score of a player for "a round of throws."*

It is easy to determine *the score* once we know what we must do. However, it takes a certain effort to present the rules by which it is calculated. To facilitate their understanding we proceed as follows:

Assume that a player, whom we shall call John, rolls the three dice. The die (or *one* of the dice) showing the highest number is set aside. The "first partial score," which we denote A, is 30 if John rolled three of a kind. Otherwise, A is the number shown on the die set aside.

John now rolls the remaining two dice. The die (or *one* of the dice) showing the highest number is set aside. The "second partial score," which we denote B, is 15 if John rolled two of a kind. Otherwise, B is the number shown on the die set aside.

Finally, John rolls the remaining die. The number produced is the "third partial score." We denote it by C.

*See the section *What about luck* in Chapter 1.

These three rolls by John form "a round of throws." The corresponding *score* is

$$A + B + C.$$

If, for instance, John rolls first (3, 3, 3), then $A = 30$. He now rolls two of the three dice. Assume he produces 5 and 1. Then $B = 5$ and the die showing 5 is set aside. The remaining die is rolled. If 6 is produced, $C = 6$. Hence, John's score for this round of throws is

$$30 + 5 + 6 = 41.$$

If, for instance, Shirley rolls the three dice and produces 4, 5 and 6, then the die showing 6 is set aside and $A = 6$. Then the dice showing 4 and 5 are rolled again. Assume she produces (4, 4).* Then $B = 15$. She now rolls one die. If she produces 1, $C = 1$. Shirley's score for this round of throws is

$$6 + 15 + 1 = 22.$$

Observe that *the largest score a player can obtain on a round of throws is*

$$30 + 15 + 6 = 51.$$

We describe next the game as played between Shirley and John.

Both players make a bet (the two bets are of equal amount). The decision as to which one of the players rolls first may be reached by tossing a coin. A die can be used instead for the same purpose.

Assume that Shirley starts rolling the three dice. She completes the first round of three throws and calculates the corresponding score, say S_1. Then John starts a round of throws

---

*If she produced instead the numbers 4 and 3, then $B = 4$.

and calculates the corresponding score, say J_1. Then Shirley starts a round of throws and calculates the second score, say S_2. At the end of the second round of throws, Shirley's *total score* is

$$S_1 + S_2.$$

Then John starts again a round of throws and calculates the corresponding score, say J_2. At this moment, John's *total score* is

$$J_1 + J_2.$$

The game continues this way *until one of the players reaches (for the first time) a total score of 100 or more. When such a score is attained, the game ends right away and the player who reached it is the winner.*

The winner collects both bets.

When played as indicated above, *the game is even.* Neither player is at a disadvantage. However, once it has been decided who starts rolling the dice, the starting player has the advantage.

It should be observed that none of the players can accumulate a total score of 100 or more in one round of throws. It is possible, although unlikely, that such a score would be reached in two rounds.

Of course, the game can be played by more than two players. However, if there are many players participating in the game and if each one of them keeps "a separate score," the game might be very long. To avoid such a situation, the persons interested in playing the game might form two groups, with each group represented by one player.

The game *Going to Boston*, described above, is also known as *Yankee Grab* or *Newmarket*.

A variant of the game is played by determining the score somewhat differently. When three of a kind is rolled, for instance, (4, 4, 4), the "first partial score" is 4, and not 30. When two of a kind is rolled, for instance, (5, 5), the "second partial score'' is 5, and not 15. When these rules are used, John's score, in the first example above, is

$$3 + 5 + 6 = 14,$$

and not 41. Shirley's score, in the second example above, is

$$6 + 4 + 1 = 11,$$

and not 22.

One more game will be discussed here, which, although played with two dice, has certain similarities with Going to Boston. We assume that the game is played between Shirley and John and that Shirley rolls the dice first.

She may roll as long as she desires, unless she produces 1 with at least one of the dice. When this happens, she must relinquish the dice to John. For instance, if the outcomes of her first four rolls are 7, 6, 12 and 4 (and none of the dice have shown 1), her *total score* is

$$7 + 6 + 12 + 4 = 29.$$

As soon as she produces 1, with at least one of the two dice, in an ''uninterrupted'' sequence of throws, her total score (accumulated during that sequence of throws) becomes zero. As was said above, when she produces 1 she must relinquish the dice. However, the rules of the game are so that she may relinquish the dice anytime she wishes; for example, after the first four rolls which gave her a score of 29. She will start a second sequence of rolls after John relinquishes the dice. The score she accumulates on this second sequence of throws is added to 29. If she throws 1, the score she accumulated on the *second sequence* of throws is cancelled (but not that accumulated during the first sequence of rolls). Shirley *must* relinquish the dice when she throws a 1. Again, she *may* relinquish the dice whenever she wishes.

The game continues this way until one of the players reaches 100 or more. If John reaches 100 or more before Shirley, the game ends right away and he is the winner (remember that it is Shirley who started rolling the dice). If Shirley reaches 100 or more and decides* to relinquish the dice, it will be John's turn to roll the dice. If he accumulates a score higher than Shirley's score before he relinquishes** the dice, he is the winner. Otherwise Shirley wins.

The win or lose decision is sometimes taken in a somewhat different manner.

Observe that the expected number of rolls (of two dice) to produce one 1 is 3.27 (hence it is "more than 3 and less than 4"). It follows that if you try to reach 100 in an "uninterrupted" sequence of throws you have an "excellent" chance to produce 1. In this case, your score will become zero and you will have to start all over again.

In the games described at the beginning of this section, the players must proceed in a predetermined way. They have no options. However, in this game, the players have the *important* choice of relinquishing the dice. Unfortunately, an optimal strategy has not yet been devised for this game. The difficulties in obtaining such a strategy are not conceptual. They are computational.

The game described above will be called *Reach 100*. Since the players have strategical options, Reach 100 is one of the most interesting games of chance played with dice. (The game is sometimes called *Pig*. I do not find "interesting" the use of this "special name." There is nothing in the structure of the game to suggest it.)

THE 4-5-6 DICE GAME

This is quite a popular game. We shall discuss it as played be-

---

*Assume that Shirley's score is 96 and on the next roll the outcome is (4, 4). Her score becomes 104. She may relinquish the dice immediately or may try to improve (?) her situation by increasing her score. Of course, she may roll a 1 and bring her score under 100.

**Obviously, John will not relinquish the dice willingly unless he has already accumulated a score higher than Shirley's score.

tween a player, Peter, and the House. The House pays Peter's wins and collects his losses.

Three dice are used in the play. An outcome of a throw of these dice is *significant* if it is one of the following types:

1. A three of a kind.
2. It consists of the numbers 4, 5 and 6.
3. It consists of the numbers 1, 2 and 3.
4. It consists of two identical numbers and a third, different one. The third number is the *point of the outcome.**

The House throws first. It rolls the three dice *until the outcome is significant.*

If the outcome is of type 1, type 2 or type 4, with point 6, the game ends and the House wins.

If the outcome is of type 3 or type 4, with point 1, the game ends and Peter wins.

The remaining possibility is that the outcome is of type 4 and the corresponding point is any one of the numbers

$$2, 3, 4 \text{ or } 5.$$

In this case, the point of the outcome becomes the *House point*. Once the House point is established, it is Peter's turn to throw the dice. He will roll *until the outcome is significant.*

If he produces an outcome of type 1, type 2 or type 4, with point 6, the game ends and Peter wins.

If the outcome is of type 3 or type 4, with point 1, the game ends and Peter loses.

If the outcome is of type 4, but different from those described above,** its point becomes *Peter's point* (or the *player's point*).

Peter wins if his point is higher than that of the House, ties if the two points are the same and loses otherwise.***

In case of a win, Peter is paid *even money*.

---

*If, for example, the throw produces *two sixes* and *a two*, the outcome is of type 4. Its point is 2.

**This means that his point is one of the numbers 2, 3, 4 or 5.

***Hence, he loses when the player's point is smaller than that of the House.

We observe that, *in a certain sense*, Peter and the House win and lose the same way. In fact, many players believe that the game is even. Since the House rolls first, this is not so. Indeed, in this game, *the House has an edge of about 2.47%.* *

More than one player may participate in the 4-5-6 dice game. For instance, assume that John, Pamela and Arlene are the players (see Fig. 5). The House** starts to throw. It rolls the dice until a significant outcome is produced. If the outcome is of type 1, type 2 or type 4, with point 6, the House wins and collects all the bets on the playing surface. If the outcome is of type 3 or type 4, with Point 1, the House loses. In this case, each one of the players is paid even money.

The remaining possibility is for the House to establish a point. In this case, John will start rolling the dice until he either wins, ties or loses (according to the rules described above). Pamela and then Arlene will do the same.

I do not like to see 4-5-6 played in this manner when several players participate in the game. It takes too long to end a round of play. If the number of players is relatively large, some of them will get bored and leave. After all, what does it matter to Arlene whether or not Pamela wins?

It is suggested, therefore, that the game be played as follows: The House throws first, rolling the three dice until the outcome is significant. If it is a winning outcome (for the House), the House collects *all* the bets on the playing surface. If it is a losing

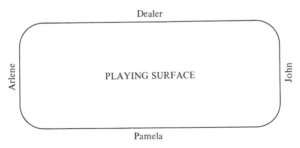

Dealer

Arlene   PLAYING SURFACE   John

Pamela

Fig. 5

*We assume that the bets are placed before the House starts rolling the dice and that they are not removed before the final decision is reached.

**The Dealer in Fig. 5 represents the House.

outcome, the House pays *each one* of the players *even money*. The remaining possibility is that the House establishes a point. In this case, a player (the Shooter) will start rolling the dice. If the Shooter's rolls result in a winning decision (for the Shooter), all the players win. If the Shooter rolls a tie or a losing decision, all the players tie or lose, respectively. Of course, the Shooter may also roll for the House.

The dice pass from one player to another according to rules similar to those in the Casino game of Craps.

When you play this game privately, you should try to assume the role of the House. If you succeed, you will make a nice profit. If the other players object, then some rule as to how to proceed is needed. For example, each one of the players may throw the three dice. If John throws the highest total, "he becomes the House." He will maintain this position until he wins twice in a row, or until he decides to relinquish the dice. The next player on his left will then become the House.

In a private game, bet small and wait your turn to play the role of the House.

THE MONTE CARLO DICE GAME

This game used to be very popular in many parts of the world, especially in Europe. Its recent decrease in popularity is probably due to the high House advantage and to the increased sophistication of many modern gamblers.

In any case, the game is still offered in various establishments, at fairs, etc. Its main attraction, for many players, is that *very high* payoffs correspond to certain bets.

The game is played with *three dice*. A layout like that shown in Fig. 6 is used. The number of players participating in the game is limited only by the space available around the table.

Below are described the kinds of bets a player can make in the Monte Carlo dice game. Observe that *all the bets on the layout either lose or win after every roll of the dice.*

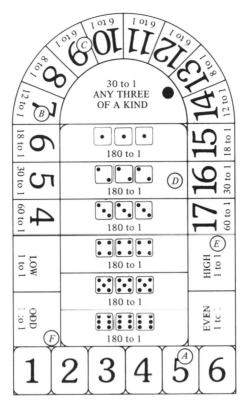

Fig. 6

Chuck-a-luck Bets

The *chuck-a-luck bets* are placed in the areas marked by the numbers 1, 2, 3, 4, 5 and 6 at the bottom of Fig. 6. The disc labeled *A* represents a *chuck-a-luck bet on 5*. If Vicki makes this bet, she will win if at *least one 5* is produced with the three dice, and will lose otherwise. The payoff for this bet is as follows:

If only one 5 is produced, Vicki is paid *even money*.
If two 5's are produced, Vicki is paid 2 to 1.
If all three dice show the number 5, Vicki is paid 3 to 1.

Of course, chuck-a-luck bets can be made on any one of the numbers 1, 2, 3, 4, 5 or 6. They are settled in the same manner.

The House advantage as far as these bets are concerned is about 7.8%.

Single Number Bets*

The disc labeled *B* and *C* in Fig. 6 represent *single number bets on 7 and 9*, respectively. If Orlando makes the bet represented by the disc *B*, he will win if 7 is produced and will lose otherwise. In case of a win, Orlando will be paid 12 to 1.

The House advantage as far as this bet is concerned is about 9.7%.

The player may place similar bets on any one of the numbers 4 to 17. The corresponding payoffs are indicated on the layout.

The House advantage for a bet on 14 is the same as that for a bet on 7. The House advantage for single number bets on 9 and 12 is about 19%. For any other single number bet, the House advantage is between 9.7% and 19%.

Hence, the best bets for the player are those on 7 and 14. The worst are those on 9 and 12.

Any Three of a kind Bets

The black disc in Fig. 6 represents an *any three of a kind bet*. If Mary makes such a bet, she wins if the outcome of the roll is one of the following triples:

(1, 1, 1), (2, 2, 2), (3, 3, 3), (4, 4, 4), (5, 5, 5), (6, 6, 6).

Otherwise she loses. In case of a win, Mary is paid 30 to 1.

The House edge in the case of these bets is about 13.8%.

Three of a kind Bets

The disc labeled *D* in Fig. 6 represents a *three of a kind bet*. If Tom places this bet, he wins if the outcome of the roll is (2, 2, 2)

---

*The *chuck-a-luck bets* described above are also "single number bets." However, they are settled differently.

and loses otherwise. In case of a win, the payoff is huge: 180 to 1.

Of course, similar bets can be made on any one of these six triples:

(1, 1, 1), (2, 2, 2), (3, 3, 3), (4, 4, 4), (5, 5, 5), (6, 6, 6).

The House advantage in the case of these bets is about 16.6%.

Bets on High and Bets on Low

The disc labeled *E* in Fig. 6 represents a *bet on high*. If Arlene places such a bet, she will win if the outcome is 11 or more and is not three of a kind. Otherwise she loses. In case of a win, Arlene is paid even money.

The player who places a *bet on low* wins if the outcome is 10 or less and is not three of a kind. Otherwise the player loses. In case of a win, the payoff is 1 to 1.

The House advantage corresponding to bets on high and bets on low is the same. It is about 2.77%.

Bets on Even and Bets on Odd

The disc labeled *F* in Fig. 6 is a *bet on odd*. This bet wins if the roll produces an odd number but not three of a kind. Otherwise the bet loses. The player who places such a bet receives even money in case of a win. A bet on even is settled in a similar manner.

The House advantage corresponding to bets on even and bets on odd is the same as that for bets on high and bets on low.

Percentagewise, the best bets for the player are those on high, low, even and odd. The next best bets are the chuck-a-luck type bets.

We do not consider the Monte Carlo game to be particularly attractive for the House. It is true that the House edge corresponding to many of the offered bets is very high, but some of the payoffs are also very high. For instance, 180 to 1, in the case of a three of a kind bet. For this reason, the game should not be offered unless the House has a substantial bankroll, the game is played a long time and the number of players is large. The fluctuations in bankroll might be great and sudden.

In any case, when the Monte Carlo game is offered, the House should impose relatively low maximum limits for three of a kind bets, any three of a kind bets and single number bets on 4, 17, 5, 16, 6 and 15.

On some of the Monte Carlo dice games layout, the word "to" is replaced by "for." For instance, in the area corresponding to a bet on 14, you will see "12 for 1" instead of "12 to 1."

When the payoff is 12 *to* 1, you are paid $12 if you bet $1 and win, and your initial bet is returned to you. Hence, if you bet $1 and win, you collect in all (your bet included) $13. When the payoff is 12 *for* 1, you collect in all (your bet included) $12. *A 12 for 1 payoff is equivalent to an 11 to 1 payoff.* This is a general custom. For example, a 180 for 1 payoff is equivalent to a 179 to 1 payoff. A 2 for 1 payoff is equivalent to a 1 to 1 payoff. (The word *for* instead of *to* is also used on many Craps layouts.)

The *Monte Carlo dice game* is also known as *Three-dice Hazard*.

CHUCK-A-LUCK

The game of *Chuck-a-luck* is essentially a particular case of the Monte Carlo dice game discussed in the previous section. Presented here is the version offered at a major Nevada Casino. Three dice and a layout like that shown in Fig. 7 are used.

The win or lose decisions depend on the outcome of the rolls of the three dice and, of course, on the bets the players make.

Chuck-a-luck Type Bets

These bets are placed in the areas marked by the numbers

1, 2, 3, 4, 5 and 6.

The bets are settled as in the case of the Monte Carlo dice game.

The House advantage as far as these bets are concerned is about 7.8%.

Field Bets

The black disc in Fig. 7 represents a field bet. The player who places such a bet wins if the outcome is one of the numbers

$$3, 4, 5, 6, 7, 13, 14, 15, 16, 17 \text{ or } 18$$

and loses otherwise. Hence, the player loses if the outcome is one of these numbers:

$$8, 9, 10, 11 \text{ or } 18.$$

In case of a win, the player is paid even money.

There are 91 ways of producing a number in the first sequence and 125 ways of producing a number in the second sequence (see the section on rolls of three dice). Since the number of all possible outcomes is 216, the probabilities to win and lose are

$$p = 91/216 \quad \text{and} \quad q = 125/216,$$

respectively. It follows that, *as far as field bets are concerned, the House has an advantage of about 15.7%*.

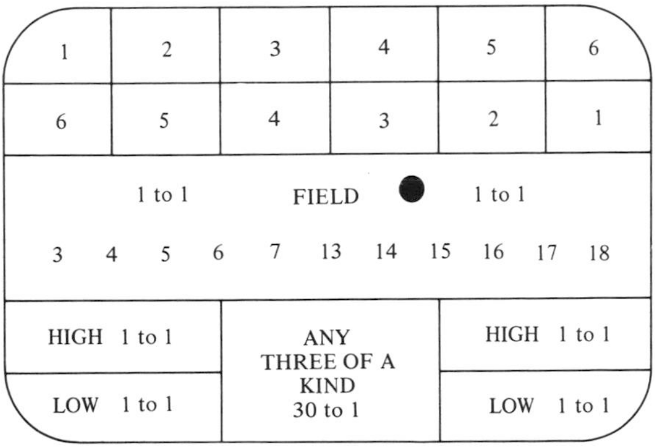

1	2	3	4	5	6
6	5	4	3	2	1

1 to 1		FIELD ●		1 to 1	
3 4 5 6	7	13 14	15	16 17 18	

HIGH 1 to 1	ANY	HIGH 1 to 1
	THREE OF A	
LOW 1 to 1	KIND 30 to 1	LOW 1 to 1

Fig. 7

High and Low Bets

The bets are settled as in the case of the Monte Carlo dice game. The payoff, in case of a win, is even money.

Recall that when you bet on high or low, the House wins if the outcome is three of a kind.

The House advantage as far as these bets are concerned is about 2.77%.

Any Three of a kind Bets

The player wins if the outcome is

$$(1, 1, 1), (2, 2, 2), (3, 3, 3), (4, 4, 4), (5, 5, 5) \text{ or } (6, 6, 6).$$

Otherwise the player loses. The payoff in case of a win is 30 to 1.

The corresponding House advantage is about 13.8%.

In conclusion, *Chuck-a-luck is a deceiving game, bad for the player.*

POKER DICE

Poker dice is played with five dice. Each one of the dice is marked with an Ace, a King, a Queen, a Jack, a Ten and a Nine.

Usual dice can be used instead in the game. In this case, 1 corresponds to an Ace, 6 to a King, 5 to a Queen, 4 to a Jack, 3 to a Ten and 2 to a Nine.

The game of Poker dice described in this section is similar to Draw Poker played with an infinity* of decks of cards mixed together (the 2's, 3's, 4's, 5's, 6's, 7's and 8's are removed from these decks). As shall be seen below, the manner in which the players bet in Poker dice is essentially different from that in Draw Poker. Also, in Poker dice we cannot differentiate between suits.

Any number of players may participate in the game. When the number of players is large, it takes a long time to arrive at a win or lose decision and hence the game might become boring.

---

*For practical purposes, this is the same as Draw Poker played with *very many* decks mixed together.

In such a case, it is suggested that the players form two or more groups which may play separately.

The game will be described as played by *four players*, whom we call Jack, John, Tom and Ted. These players are seated at a table as shown in Fig. 8. Each player places an equal amount in the "pot." One of the players, for example Jack, starts the play* by rolling the five dice. If he does not like the outcome, he may set aside whichever he wants of the five dice and roll again the remaining ones. By the rules of the game, he may roll at most three of the five dice the second time. *Jack's hand* consists of the symbols on the dice set aside after the first roll and those produced on the second roll.

If, for example, Jack produced 9, 9, A, 10, Q, he may set aside the two 9's and the Ace and roll again the dice showing 10 and Q. If he produces one Ace and a Nine on the second roll, *his hand* is

$$9, 9, 9, A, A.$$

Once Jack's hand is determined, it is John's turn to roll the dice. He proceeds the same way Jack did. Once John's hand is established, it is Tom's turn and then, finally, it is Ted's turn to roll the dice.

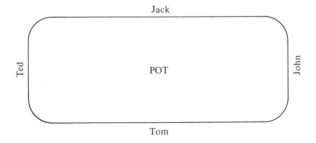

Fig. 8

*The players' seating and the starting player should be decided by some rule agreed upon by those participating in the game. When reading the description of the game given below, note that, when the players are seated as in Fig. 8, Ted has the advantage of knowing the hands of the other players before he decides how to proceed on the second roll. I suggest that, if Jack starts "the first round of play," John should start "the second round of play," etc.

When the hands of all players are established, they are compared and the player holding the highest hand is the winner. The winner collects the total amount in the pot.*

The hands in Poker dice are ranked more or less as in Draw Poker. In any case, for completeness, the ranking of the hands is described here in detail (the hand described first is higher than that described second; the one described second is higher than that described third; etc).

1. *Five of a kind.* Five Aces beat five Kings, five Kings beat five Queens, etc.
2. *Four of a kind.* For example, a hand consisting of 10, 10, 10, 10, K is four of a kind. Four Aces beat four Kings, four Kings beat four Queens, etc. If two hands consist of the same four of a kind, then the "fifth" dice decides the winner. For instance, J, J, J, J, A beats J, J, J, J, Q, etc.
3. *Full house.* A *full house* is a hand consisting of three of one kind and two of another. For example,

   A, A, A, 9, 9   10, 10, 10, K, K   J, J, J, Q, Q

   are full houses. Of two full houses, the hand containing the higher three of a kind is the winner. For instance, J, J, J, 9, 9 beats 10, 10, 10, A, A. If both hands contain the same three of a kind, the remaining cards decide the winner. For example, A, A, A, 9, 9 is beaten by A, A, A, J, J.
4. *High straight* is the hand A, K, Q, J, 10.
5. *Low straight* is the hand K, Q, J, 10, 9.
6. *Three of a kind.* Of two such hands, the one containing the higher three of a kind wins. If two hands contain the same three of a kind, "the other" two dice are used to decide the winner. The following examples show how the decision is taken: The hand J, J, J, A, 9 beats J, J, J, K, Q; the hand J, J, J, A, Q beats J, J, J, A, 10; the hand A, A, A, J, 9 beats A, A, A, 10, 9; the hand A, A, A, J, 10 beats A, A, A, J, 9.

---

*When several players hold the same highest hand, the pot is split equally between these players.

7. *Two pairs.* Of two such hands, the one with the higher pair wins. For instance K, K, 10, 10, 9 beats Q, Q, J, J, A. If the higher pairs are the same in both hands, the *other* pairs decide the winner. For instance, K, K, 10, 10, 9 beats K, K, 9, 9, A. If both pairs are the same, the winner is decided by the remaining die. For example, Q, Q, J, J, K beats Q, Q, J, J, 10.

8. *One pair.* Of two such hands, the one having the higher pair wins. For example, J, J, Q, 9, 10 beats 9, 9, K, Q, A. When the two hands contain the same pair, the "highest symbol" on the other three dice decides the winner. For instance, 9, 9, A, J, 10 beats 9, 9, K, Q, J (observe that the "highest symbol" shown by the other three dice in the first hand is A and in the second hand is K). The same principle is used when these "highest symbols" are the same. For instance, 9, 9, A, K, 10 beats 9, 9, A, Q, J. Also, 9, 9, A, K, J beats 9, 9, A, K, 10.

A hand which does not belong to any of the categories listed above is said to be *indifferent.* An indifferent hand does not contain two of a kind and is not a straight. An indifferent hand is beaten by any of the hands in the categories listed above. Two indifferent hands are not comparable; that is, none beats the other. If *all the players* participating in the game have indifferent hands, the "pot" remains untouched, and a new round of play is started by the same player.

Observe that the probability of rolling two pairs with five dice is about 0.23. The probability of rolling a full house or "better" is about 6/100. The probability of starting with two pairs and obtaining as a final hand a full house is 1/3. Other probabilities of this type can be readily computed.

Assume, as we did above, that Jack starts the game. In this case, Tom must proceed so as to maximize the probability that he beats Jack's and John's hands and is not beaten or tied by Ted. This is, of course, Tom's *optimal* strategy. Such strategies can be devised for Poker dice,* but the corresponding computations are laborious.

*The corresponding problem for Draw Poker is much more difficult.

Poker dice can be played according to rules somewhat different than those described above. The ranking of the hands may be modified. For instance, two hands such as

K, K, K, K, 10 and K, K, K, K, Q

may be considered equal. One other usual modification is to have the players tying for the highest hand replay the round, instead of splitting the pot. However, for various reasons, I prefer to play Poker dice according to the rules described in detail in this section. In particular, when played according to these rules, the game moves faster.

A somewhat similar game is *Indian Poker*, known also as *Indian dice*. The main differences between this game and Poker dice are the following:

1. In Indian Poker, a player is allowed three rolls of the dice to establish the final hand (in Poker dice, the player may roll, at most, twice). The players may roll each time as many dice as he/she wishes (in Poker dice, the player may throw, at most, three dice on the second roll).
2. Straights are considered as indifferent hands.
3. Aces are wild (this means that an Ace can replace any symbol or number the player wants).

GENERAL

The game is played with five dice. As many players as can sit around the playing surface may participate in the game. However, if the number of players is very large, it will take a long time to determine the winner.

In this section, we assume that the game is played by four players, whom we call Orlando, Maria, Jack and Robert (see Fig. 9).

The game consists of *ten rounds*,* which in a sense corre-

*The term "frame" instead of "round" is often used.

Fig. 9

spond to the *categories* listed in the first column of the score sheet (see Fig. 10).

In every round, each player *scores* a number of points. The result is recorded on the *scoring sheet* (see Fig. 10). The score depends on the player's *final hand* in the corresponding round.

To determine his *final hand*, Orlando rolls the five dice. The outcome of the throw is his final hand *if he so decides*. If he does not like the outcome, he may set aside whichever he wants of the five dice and roll the remaining ones (by the rules of the game, he may again roll as many dice as he likes). The hand obtained after the second roll is his final hand *if he so decides*. If he is not satisfied with the new hand, he sets aside whichever he wants of the dice he threw the second time and rolls the remaining ones (a die, once set aside, *cannot* be rolled again). *Whatever the third roll is, the hand produced now is final.* By the rules of the game, he cannot throw the dice a fourth time.

For instance, assume that Orlando produced 6, 6, 6, 5, 1 on his first roll, in the fourth round. He sets aside the three dice showing 6 and rolls the remaining two. Assume he produces 6 and 2. He sets aside the die showing 6 and rolls that showing 2 again. Assume he produces 5. His final hand is 6, 6, 6, 6, 5.

It is important to observe that whether or not a hand obtained after the first or second roll is final depends on Orlando's decision. *There is, however, an important exception.* When a player produces *five of a kind* on the first roll, the hand is final and the game ends right away (this case is discussed further in this section).

The other players participating in the game determine their final hands, in each round, in the same way.

A *four of a kind** on the first roll has a value of 45 points. If two or three rolls are needed to obtain such a hand, its value is only 40 points. For example, if, in the fourth round, Jack obtains a four of a kind on the first roll, the hand counts 45 points.

A *full house* on the first roll has a value of 30 points. If two or three rolls are needed to obtain such a hand, its value is only 25 points.

A *straight* on the first roll has a value of 25 points. If two or three rolls are needed to obtain such a hand, its value is only 20 points. The Aces (that is, the 1's) may be counted 1, 2 or 6, when the player wants to produce a straight. Notice that this is the only case when Aces may be counted this way. For example, the hand 6, 6, 6, A, 5 is *not* four of a kind. The hand 5, 5, 2, 2, A is *not* a full house.

The *highest hand* in the game is the *great general*. It consists of *five of a kind* produced on a *first throw*. If, for example, in the seventh round, Robert's first roll has for an outcome a *five of a kind*, he produced a *great general. In this case, the game ends right away and he is declared the winner.*** Robert will receive a certain amount of money from the other players (we assume, of course, that the game is played for money, the only thing to which most of our present society seems to attribute any value). The amount to be paid a player who rolls a great general should be agreed upon before the start of the game.

A *five of a kind* obtained on the second or third roll is not a great general. It is called a *little general* and has a value of 60 points.

We may now see how an actual game proceeds.

Orlando rolls the five dice.*** If he produces a great general,

---

*See the section on Poker dice.

*We assume that no great general was previously produced.

***Who starts the rounds and the players' positions around the table should be decided by some rule agreed upon by those participating in the game. If Orlando starts the first round of throws, I prefer to see Maria start the second round, Jack the third round, Robert the fourth round, Orlando the fifth, etc.

the game ends and Orlando is the winner. Otherwise, he rolls the dice until his final hand is determined. Then he chooses a category and records in the obvious place on the scoring sheet (Fig. 10) the corresponding score. If, for instance, the final hand is a little general and the player chooses the little general category, 60 points will be recorded on the scoring sheet. If the final hand is four of a kind and the player chooses the same

	Orlando	Maria	Jack	Robert
Little general				
Four of a kind				
Full house				
Straight				
Six				
Five				
Four				
Three				
Two				
Ace				
Total				

Scoring Sheet*

Fig. 10

*The maximum scores which can be recorded in each category are as follows: little general, 60; four of a kind, 45; full house, 35; straight, 25; six, 30; five, 25; four, 20; three, 15; two, 10; and Aces, 5.

category, 45 or 40 points are recorded on the scoring sheet (the exact score depends on the number of rolls needed to produce the final hand). If the final hand is *four of a kind* and the player chooses the category *straight*, the score recorded on the sheet will be zero. (If you read the rest of this section, you will see why a player might have to make such a choice.) If Orlando's final hand is 6, 6, 6, 5, 4 and he chooses the category *six*, he records the score 18 (= 3 × 6). If he chooses the category *five*, he records the score 5 (= 1 × 5). If he chooses the category *four*, he records the score 4 (= 1 × 4). If he chooses any other category, he must record a score equal to zero.

One very important rule the players must always remember is the following: *A player cannot choose the same category twice.* This explains why choices which give a zero score must be sometimes made. For example, assume that Orlando rolled a *little general* in the fourth round and that he recorded 60 points in the same category. Assume now that he produces 5, 5, 5, 5, 5 in the seventh round. By the rule mentioned above, he cannot choose the *little general* category and record 60 points. He must choose the category *five, if it is available,* and record a score equal to 25 (= 5 × 5). However, if the category *Five* was already chosen in a previous round, he will have to record a score equal to zero, no matter what category he chooses. In such a case, it might be convenient to choose the category *Ace,* if available.

Once Orlando's score is recorded, Maria proceeds the same way and records her score. Then it is Jack's turn and then, finally, Robert's turn to roll the dice and determine their respective scores.

Once Robert's score is recorded, a new round starts. The game continues this way until all ten rounds are completed.*

The *total score* for each player is determined by adding the scores obtained in the ten rounds. The player having the highest score is the *winner*. The winner is paid, as explained in the following example: Assume Orlando's total score is 240, Maria's total score is 210, Jack's total score is 160 and Robert's total score is 212. If the game is played at $1 *per point*, Orlando receives:

---

*Of course, the game might end sooner if a player produces a great general.

$30 (30 = 240 − 210) from Maria;
$80 (80 = 240 − 160) from Jack;
$28 (28 = 240 − 212) from Robert.

Hence, he gains $138. Notice that if the game were played at $20 per point, Orlando would have won $2760.

If two or more players tie for the highest score, we recommend that the settlement be made as explained in the following example: Assume Orlando and Maria have a total score of 240 points. Assume Jack's total score is 140 and Robert's total score is 201. If the game is played at $1 *per point*, Orlando and Maria together receive:

$100 (100 = 240 − 140) from Jack;
$39 (39 = 240 − 201) from Robert.

Hence, Orlando and Maria will gain $69.50 each.

Recall that, by the rules above, whether or not a hand obtained after the first or second roll is final depends on the player's decision. Also, a player may choose whatever category he/she wants (for recording a score), no matter what the hand is. For various reasons, I prefer to see the game played according to these rules. However, the following rules are sometimes adopted: If Maria, say, produced on the first or second roll a four of a kind, a full house, a straight or a little general, she *cannot* roll again. Also, when she produces one of the four hands mentioned above, she *must* choose the same category, if available. If the corresponding category is not available, she may choose any other available category. For example, if, on the first roll in the third round, she produces 2, 2, 2, 2, 1, she must choose four of a kind and record 45 points on the scoring sheet. Observe that Maria has the probability

$$11/36 = \text{about } 0.3$$

of obtaining a little general if she were allowed to roll twice more. Hence, about a third of the time she proceeds this way she would improve her hand. Such a strategy might be much better than the one she is forced to follow ("standing" on her hand), especially if the category four of a kind is not available while the little general is.

3. Probability, Expectation and Gambling Systems

We begin this chapter with a brief examination of probabilities and expectations. These ideas are basic to the study of all problems about games of chance. We can use them to determine who has the advantage in a game. More precisely, by using the idea of expectation, we can make very precise estimations of the size of the advantage.

Gamblers who have some knowledge of probability and expectation have a better understanding of the games they are playing and, therefore, will be more successful. It is *nonsense* to say that "once you decide to gamble, it makes no difference what games you play, since, if you are 'lucky,' you will win anyhow." I am ready to play the part of the House in a game of Craps, for example, against *any players,* no matter how "lucky" or how "hot" they are!

To say that the probability of an event A is, for instance, 15/100 means that it is as likely for A to occur as it is to select a green ball from a box containing 15 green and 85 red balls.*

The meaning of "percent advantage," which is computed using expectations, can also be explained in a very simple way. For example, to say that the House has a 1.41% advantage against the players who bet on the line means that, in the long run, the House takes 1.41% of the total amount placed as pass line bets.

---

*We assume, of course, that all the balls in the box have, except for color, the same characteristics.

It is important to realize that the House takes 1.41% of the money *placed on the table*, not of the money the players have in their pockets or, maybe, in their bank accounts in Switzerland.

An understanding of the above remarks is useful (though not absolutely essential) for the reading of certain parts of this volume. We suggest that *every* gambler read the section discussing the gambler's ruin formula (and several of its consequences) and the remarks on "bold" play in the last section of this chapter.

PROBABILITY

If a box contains, for example, 5 balls, all of them having the same characteristics (that is size, weight, etc.) and if we decide to pick one of them, then each one of the five balls is as likely to be selected as any other. We say that the *probability* that any particular ball in the box will be selected is 1/5.

When an element is chosen from a finite set (or *collection*) X, in such a way that every object is equally likely to be selected, the probability $P(A)$ that the selected object is from a *subset A* of X is given by

$$P(A) = \frac{\text{Number of elements of } A}{\text{Number of elements of } X} . \tag{1}$$

Put another way, the probability of the *event* which consists of selecting a ball from the subset A, an event which we shall denote again by the letter A, is given by (1).

The probability $P(A)$ measures the likelihood that A will occur. The larger $P(A)$ is, the more likely it is that the event A will occur. This is quite obvious if we notice that $P(A)$ increases when the number of elements in A increases, and that the larger the number of elements of A is, the more likely it is that the chosen object be from A.

If the balls in the box mentioned above have the same characteristics *except* that two are green and three are red, then the probability that the selected ball will be green is 2/5. In fact, in this case, we may assume X to be the set of all balls in X, and

A the subset consisting of the green balls. Since *X* has 5 elements and *A* has 2 elements, (1) gives

$$P(A) = 2/5.$$

Now assume that we perform *n* successive selections from the box (we place the ball back in the box after each selection) and that *k* is the number of times the chosen ball was green. Hence, *k* is the number of times the event *A*, consisting of the selection of a green ball, has occurred during the *n* trials. Then the fraction

$$\frac{k}{n}$$

is termed *the frequency of the event in the series of n trials.*

It is an extremely important experimental fact (and this is what makes for the importance of probability theory in so many and such varied application) that the larger the number n is, the more likely it is for k/n to be close to the probability of A. Hence, we may say that the frequency of the event approximates its probability.

Of course, we may introduce in the same way the frequency of other events of the same or a more general type.

In certain cases, we may even deduce what the probability of an event is, or at least find an approximate value of its probability, by using its *frequency*. For instance, assume again that we have a box containing 5 balls, 2 green and 3 red, but that this time the balls are quite different. What is the probability that, if we pick a ball from the box (obviously, without looking inside), the selected one will be green? *Since we want the probability to indicate a practical measure of the chance of selecting a green ball, we cannot say anymore that it is 2/5.* For example, if the green balls are very large when compared with the red balls, it is likely that we shall always be selecting green balls. How do we estimate the probability of the event *A*, which consists of the selection of a green ball?

A usual method is to make a long series of selections, to count the number of times k the event A occurs and to use the frequency k/n as the probability of A.

We observe that the setting described at the beginning of this section is general and can be used for discussing many other various problems. The selection of an object from a finite set X can also be performed in many ways. For example, consider a die. Let X be the set of the 6 symbols 1, 2, . . . , 6. We may decide to choose an object from X by the following method: We roll the die, and, if after the roll, the number facing upward is (for instance) 2, we say that 2 has been selected from X. It should be quite obvious that, if the die is honest, the probability that any one of the six objects in X is selected is 1/6.

The reader should remember that *whenever we use formula (1), we must assume that every object in X is equally likely to be selected.*

As one more example, we shall determine *the probability of producing two heads in two tosses of a coin.* In this problem, the set X consists of all possible outcomes corresponding to our "experiment," and hence it consists of the *pairs*

(tail, tail), (tail, head), (head, head), (head, tail).

If the coin is honest, these four outcomes are equally likely to occur. The event which consists of tossing two heads is represented by the set A, containing only the pair (head, head). Since A has only one element and X four, formula (1) gives

$$P(A) = 1/4.$$

Hence, the probability of tossing two heads is 1/4.

In the last part of the second section of Chapter 1, we discussed the above problem and indicated that Jean D'Alembert obtained a *wrong value* for this probability. It is interesting to explain how he tried to solve the problem. He assumed that there are only three cases to be considered, namely: 1) the case when tail occurs on the first toss,* 2) the case when head is tossed first and then tail and 3) the case when two heads are

---

*Notice that, in this case, it is no longer possible to obtain two heads.

tossed. He concluded *wrongly* that the probability of tossing two heads is 1/3.

It is true that when you toss a coin twice, one of the above three cases must occur. However, *these three cases are not equally likely to occur. Hence, one cannot conclude that the probability that case three occurs is 1/3.*

If D'Alembert had performed a series of *two tosses of a coin*, he would have observed that the *frequency* of occurrence of the first case is close to 1/2 and the *frequency* of occurrence of each one of the other two cases is 1/4.

I have not presented the above example in order to criticize D'Alembert. In fact, I hesitated to introduce this discussion here. After all, Jean D'Alembert made substantial contributions to the progress of science. I wanted, however, to impress upon the reader that even very simple probability problems should be treated very carefully. One should not base conclusions on quick "intuitive" considerations. Those who like to proceed in this manner should read again some of the games discussed in Chapter 2. They should also read the section on the birthday paradox in this chapter.

Here we notice that in certain cases we may have to consider experiments leading to an *infinity* of possible events. The probability cannot be defined anymore by (1) in such situations (for instance, we cannot perform the division in that formula). However, the frequency of an event can still be defined and used to estimate its probability.

Even for the study of certain dice problems which *might seem* very simple, it is necessary to introduce "infinite models." Of course, we can use "finite models" and formula (1) for computing the probability of rolling 7 or 6, etc. However, we cannot, for example, *prove*, using "finite models," that the probability of rolling 9 before 7 is 4/10.

CERTAIN PROBABILITIES IN THE GAME OF CRAPS

When you *roll two dice*, 36 different outcomes are possible. It is easy to understand this is we assume that one of the dice is *green* and the other *red*. If, for example, 3 is rolled with the white die

Table 1.

(1, 6)	(2, 6)	(3, 6)	(4, 6)	(5, 6)	(6, 6)
(1, 5)	(2, 5)	(3, 5)	(4, 5)	(5, 5)	(6, 5)
(1, 4)	(2, 4)	(3, 4)	(4, 4)	(5, 4)	(6, 4)
(1, 3)	(2, 3)	(3, 3)	(4, 3)	(5, 3)	(6, 3)
(1, 2)	(2, 2)	(3, 2)	(4, 2)	(5, 2)	(6, 2)
(1, 1)	(2, 1)	(3, 1)	(4, 1)	(5, 1)	(6, 1)

and 1 with the red one, we say that the outcome is (3, 1). The set of all possible outcomes is given in Table 1.

If the dice are honest, these 36 outcomes are equally likely to occur.

As we have seen in Chapters 1 and 2, most of the time we are interested not directly in the pair of numbers we produced, but in their sum. Inspecting Table 1, we see that:

Table 2.

2 can be rolled only in one way (namely, (1, 1)).
12 can be rolled only in one way (namely, (6, 6)).
3 and 11 can (each) be rolled only in two ways.
4 and 10 can (each) be rolled only in three ways.
5 and 9 can (each) be rolled only in four ways.
6 and 8 can (each) be rolled only in five ways.
7 can be rolled in six ways.

From Table 2 and formula (1), we deduce that, when we roll two dice, the probability of producing 7 is 6/36 = 1/6.

In the same way, we compute the probabilities of producing 4, 5, 6, 8, 9 and 10. These probabilities are listed below in Table 3. (For any number a we denote $P(a)$ the probability of rolling the sum a.)

*Tables 1 and 2 were given in Chapter 1. They are given here again to facilitate reference.

Table 3.

$$P(4) \; = \; P(10) \; = \; \frac{3}{36} \; = \; \frac{1}{12}$$

$$P(5) \; = \; P(9) \; = \; \frac{4}{36} \; = \; \frac{1}{9}$$

$$P(6) \; = \; P(8) \; = \; \frac{5}{36}$$

From any one of the above three tables, we deduce that, in the usual game of Craps, a point can be produced in *24 ways* on come-out rolls. It follows that *the probability of establishing a point is*

$$\frac{24}{36} \; = \; \frac{2}{3} \; .$$

Hence, in the long run, *about two-thirds of the come-out rolls produce a point.*

When we play Craps and a point is established, the dice continue to be rolled until either 7 or the point is thrown. The following list of probabilities (Table 4) is therefore of interest. (For any two numbers a, b, we denote $P(a, b)$ the probability of rolling a before b.)

It follows that *the best points* for the players who wager on the pass line are 6 and 8. The *worst* are 4 and 10.

To establish the values of the probabilities in Table 4 is not easy. Complete proofs require the use of "infinite models." For this reason, they will not be included here. (The interested reader may consult *A Book on Casino Gambling,*[14] pp. 145–146.)

In any case, once the probabilities in Table 4 are known, it is

Table 4.

$$P(6, 7) = P(8, 7) = 5/11 \quad P(7, 6) = P(7, 8) = 6/11$$
$$P(4, 7) = P(10, 7) = 3/9 \quad P(7, 4) = P(7, 10) = 6/9$$
$$P(5, 7) = P(9, 7) = 4/10 \quad P(7, 5) = P(7, 9) = 6/10$$

relatively easy to compute various other probabilities; *for example, the probability of winning a pass line bet.* Without going into details, we observe that this probability has the value

$$\textit{Probability of rolling 7 or 11}$$

$$+ \; P(4)P(4, 7) \; + \; P(5)P(5, 7) \; + \; P(6)P(6, 7)$$

$$+ \; P(8)P(8, 7) \; + \; P(9)P(9, 7) \; + \; P(10)P(10, 7).$$

The probability of rolling 7 or 11 is 8/36. Using this value and Tables 3 and 4, we obtain *for the probability of winning a pass line bet the value*

$$\frac{976}{1980} = 0.4929292 \ldots = \text{about } 0.49292.$$

Other probabilities of interest to Craps players (especially to those who play in private games) can be found in the section on Probabilities and fair payoffs in Craps, in Chapter 1.

EXPECTATION

The concept of *expectation* discussed in this section (in a somewhat special setting) is *of great interest for evaluating gains and losses in all sorts of situations.* These situations do not have to be directly related with betting in games of chance. For example, expectation is used by insurance companies to determine the prices charged for their policies. The probabilities used in the corresponding computations are obtained from various accident statistics. Expectations are also used by stock market analysts to evaluate investments.

To understand the concept of expectation, consider this simple example: A box contains a number of balls, some of them *white* and the rest *red*. Let p be the probability of selecting a white ball and q that of selecting a red ball. Assume now that we play the following game in a Casino: A ball is selected from the box. If the ball is white, we receive $5. If it is red, we pay $2.*

---

*The $2 is, in fact, *the bet* we "invested" in the game.

By definition, our *mathematical expectation* (or simply *expectation*) *in this game* is

$$E = 5p + (-2)q.$$

As we shall see from the discussion below, *the game is favorable for us when E > 0, it is fair* when E = 0 and it is unfavorable when E < 0.***

Assume, for instance, that

$$p = \frac{4}{10} \text{ and } q = \frac{6}{10}.$$

Then

$$E = 5\frac{4}{10} + (-2)\frac{6}{10} = 0.8.$$

By the remarks above, the game is favorable to us. *Let us see why.*

Since the probability of selecting a white ball is 4/10, in every ten games we expect to select four white balls.*** Hence, in every ten games we expect to receive

$$4 \times \$5 = \$20.$$

In the same way, we see that in every ten games we expect to lose

$$6 \times \$2 = \$12.$$

---

*Instead of *fair*, we may say *even*. When the game is fair, neither side has any advantage.

**The symbol ">" means *greater*. The symbol "<" means *smaller*. A number M is *positive* if $M > 0$. A number Q is *negative* if $Q < 0$. If $M > 0$, then $-M < 0$, and conversely. We have $0.5 > 0$, $3 > 0$, $-0.2 < 0$ and $-1 < 0$. We have $4 - 3 = 1$ and $3 - 4 = -1$. We have $0.5 - 0.3 = 0.2$ and $0.3 - 0.5 = -0.2$. The notations $a + (-b)$ and $a - b$ have the same meaning.

We cannot go into many other details here. Observe, however, that without using a minimum of mathematical symbolism it is practically impossible to present some of the most elementary results pertaining to gambling (for instance, the very important *ruin formula*, which will be given in a later section).

***This means that, in the long run, we select white balls about *four-tenths* of the time.

Therefore, in every ten games, we expect to gain

$$\$20 - \$12 = \$8.$$

We deduce that, in the long run, we have a gain of $8/10 (that is, $0.8) per game (notice that 0.8 is the value of our expectation in this game). To participate in the game, we placed a $2 bet. We deduce that, in the long run, a $2 investment brings a gain of $0.8. Hence, a $1 investment brings a gain of

$$\$0.8/2 = \$0.4.$$

A $100 investment brings a gain of $40.

We conclude that in this game we have an advantage of 40%.

What a nice game to play! What a pity that any Casino offering it will quickly go broke.

If the 5 to 2 payoff is changed to 2.5 to 2 (that is, if we receive $2.50 when the selected ball is white and pay $2 when it is red), then

$$E = (2.5)\frac{4}{10} + (-2)\frac{6}{10} = 0.$$

In the same way as above, we see that, in this case, $1 invested in the game brings "a gain" of zero dollars. *Hence, this game is fair.*

Finally, assume that the payoff is 1 to 1; that is, we receive $1 when the selected ball is white and pay $1 when it is red. Then

$$E = 1\frac{4}{10} + (-1)\frac{6}{10} = -0.2.$$

Reasoning as in the case when the payoff was 5 to 2, we see that this time we lose* $0.2 per game. Since we have invested a $1 bet, it follows that we lose $0.2 per dollar. Hence, in this

---

*Instead of saying that we lose $0.2 per game, we may say that we gain $-\$0.2$ per game. Hence, a "negative gain" is really a loss. Observe that -0.2 is the value of the expectation.

case, we lose—in the long run, about $20 of every $100 invested in the game.

We conclude that this time we have a 20% disadvantage. Our "opponent" has a 20% advantage.

If we play this game 1000 times and each time wager $10, we shall certainly lose about $2000. There is no doubt whatsoever about this.

Note that we have the advantage when $E > 0$ and the disadvantage when $E < 0$. The game is fair when $E = 0$.

Similar conclusions hold for all sorts of similar games.

Also observe that the expectation E, multiplied by 100 and divided by the amount bet per game (in the first situation, this amount was $2), is the percent advantage or disadvantage.

The remaining part of this section is for the reader with theoretical inclinations.

We shall define now the concept of expectation in the case of somewhat more general games. Let

$$X_1, X_2, \ldots, X_n$$

n be incompatible* events which may occur as a result of a certain experiment. Assume also that one of these events *must* occur. Let $p_1, p_2, \ldots, p_n$ be the corresponding probabilities of $X_1, X_2, \ldots, X_n$. If we are paid $\$y_i$ when X_i $(i = 1, 2, \ldots, n)$ occurs, then our expectation in this game is

$$E = y_1p_1 + y_2p_2 + \ldots + y_np_n.$$

Here, y_i might be > 0, might be 0, or might be < 0. If, say, y_3 is < 0, this means that we pay $\$(-y_3)$ when X_3 occurs. Again, the player has the advantage when $E > 0$ and the disadvantage when $E < 0$. The game is fair when $E = 0$.

We close this section with a few remarks concerning "the odds in favor of an event." Let A be an event, the probability of

---

*This means that $X_1, X_2, \ldots, X_n$ cannot occur at the same time. For instance, when tossing a die, the event consisting of producing 1 or 2 and that consisting of producing 4 or 6 are obviously incompatible.

occurrence of which is p. The probability that A does not occur is then $1 - p$.

We say that *the odds in favor of A are r to s if*

$$\frac{r}{s} = \frac{p}{1 - p}.$$

For example, if A consists of producing 6 when rolling one die, $p = 1/6$. Hence, $p/(1 - p) = 1/5$. It follows that *the odds in favor of producing 6 when rolling one die are 1 to 5.* Observe that we may also say that *the odds in favor of producing 6 when rolling one die are 2 to 10, or 3 to 15 or 20 to 100, etc.*

Notice that if we receive \$5 when producing 6 and pay \$1 otherwise, our expectation in "this game" is

$$5\frac{1}{6} - \frac{5}{6} = 0.$$

Hence, the game is fair.

A similar remark is valid in general. If the odds in favor of A are r to s, then if we receive \$s when A occurs and pay \$r otherwise, the game is fair.*

THE BIRTHDAY PARADOX

We will examine this paradox for several reasons. First, it is an interesting example related to probability and expectation. Second, the final conclusions are quite unexpected. This shows again that our "intuition" may lead to wrong decisions. Finally, the discussion below suggests a game of chance we can play with a *huge* advantage.

We assume that Barbara is at a party and that she proposes to Denny, one of the guests, that they play the following game: "Let's check the birthdays (*day and month only*) of all the guests here, and if at least two of them have *the same birthday*, you pay me \$10. Otherwise I will pay you \$10."

---

*See also the formula given in the section on Probabilities and fair payoffs in Craps, in Chapter 1.

Most people believe that this game cannot be favorable for Barbara unless the party is very, very large. Since in a year there are 365 days,* many believe that for the game to be favorable to Barbara there should be more than

$$182 \ (182.5 \ = \ 365/2)$$

guests at the party.

However, this is not the case. *With only 23 persons at the party, the game becomes favorable to Barbara.*

When 25 guests are at the party, Barbara's advantage is more than 13%. Remember that this means that she is expected to make a profit equal to more than 13% of the amount she wages in the game.

When 30 or 40 persons are at the party, Barbara has a *huge* advantage. *If she is "a party goer" and finds "friends" to play the game with, she will make a small fortune.*

Her edge in the game can be easily determined from the data in Table 5. The numbers in the first column represent the

Table 5.

5	0.027
10	0.117
15	0.253
18	0.347
20	0.411
21	0.444
22	0.476
23	0.507
24	0.538
25	0.569
27	0.627
30	0.706
35	0.814
40	0.891
50	0.970
60	0.995
70	0.999

*We "neglect" February 29.

number of persons at the party (or in the group we consider). The numbers in the second column are the probabilities that at least two persons in the considered group have the same birthday.

Barbara will have the advantage as soon as the probabilities in the second column become greater than 0.5 (= 1/2). When 30 persons are at the party, her probability of winning is greater than 7/10. When 40 persons are at the party, her probability of winning is almost 9/10.

Expressed in percentages, her advantage is as follows:

30 persons at the party—over 40% advantage.
40 persons at the party—almost 80% advantage.

We observe that, when there are 40 persons (or more) in the group we consider, Barbara's advantage is huge, even if she is paid 1 to 3 in case of a win. In fact, since the probability that she wins is 0.891, her expected gain per every three dollars invested as a bet is

$$1 \times 0.891 - 3 \times 0.109 = 0.564$$

Hence, her advantage is about 19%.

You do not have to be at a large party to play this game. You might be able to play it even at a small "friendly" gathering. If, for instance, your host has a *Who's Who in America*, you may start by saying that you believe that "great men and women are born during certain periods of the year." Of course, this does not make much sense, but we assume that your purpose is not to make sense—it is to make a profit. In any case, to explain what you "really mean," offer to bet even money that if you choose at random a "very small group" of persons listed in *Who's Who*—for example, 35 or 40—at least two must have the same birthday. If somebody bites the hook, you will have a nice profit for the evening, since, using a *Who's Who*, you might be able to play the game many times in a row.

WHAT CHANCE HAS A PLAYER TO WIN $100 WHEN MAKING PASS LINE BETS? THE GAMBLER'S RUIN FORMULA

John is in a Casino, ready to enter a game of Craps. He has decided to make pass line bets.* John read the first chapter of this book and knows, therefore, that the House has an edge of about 1.41%. However, he is an optimist and hopes to end a winner. *How justified is his hope?*

Fortunately, we may show that if John's capital is large enough and if the sum he wants to win is reasonable, he has a considerable chance of success.

The relation between "desired gain" and "capital" will appear clearly in the several striking cases described below. Our discussion is based on the famous *gambler's ruin formula*. Since this formula requires a certain mathematical symbolism, it is given at the end of this section. In the examples below, the results obtained on the basis of the formula are given. The calculations necessary for obtaining these results are not included here.

I

Assume that John has $1000 and that he wants to win $100. He places pass line bets of $100 each. It is important to remember that we assume John plays until he either loses the $1000 or gains $100. If this "rule" is not followed, the conclusions below are not valid.

On the basis of the gambler's ruin formula, we deduce that the probability that John reaches his goal is about 9/10.** This means that, on the average, 9 out of 10 players proceeding as John does will make $100. The remaining one will lose $1000.

Instead of placing bets of $100, John might want to make $10 bets. It is interesting to observe that, if his capital and goal are the same as before, his probability of success is now only about 0.75. This means that, on the average, about three-quarters of

*To simplify, we assume that he makes bets of equal amounts.
**More precisely, this probability is about 0.89569.

the players proceeding as John does will make $100. The remaining ones will be ruined.*

In fact, a more general conclusion holds: If John's capital is $1000 and his goal is to gain $100, he has the greatest chance of success when he places bets of $100. If he decreases the size of his bets, the chance that he will be ruined increases.**

II

Assume that John is in Las Vegas, that *he has $5000 in his pocket and that he wants to win $500,* so that he can cover his round trip first class plane fare from Chicago. In this case, we can show that if he proceeds as indicated in the case discussed above, he will again have a probability of success of about 9/10.

Notice that

$$10 \times 100 = 1000 \text{ and } 10 \times 500 = 5000.$$

In fact, any time your capital is *ten times* the amount you want to win (and this amount is not greater than the maximum bet limit), the probability of achieving success is about 9/10.†

III

Assume that *John has $20,000 in his pocket and that he wants to make $1000.* He is in a posh Casino and he is allowed to make $1000 pass line bets. In this case, the probability of success is about 94/100.†† Hence, on the average, about 94¶ out of any group of 100 players will gain $1000. The remaining ones will each lose $20,000. Notice that this does not mean the Casino will lose. In fact, the above conclusions show that, on the

*That is, will lose the $1000.
**See also the last section of this Chapter.
†We assume, of course, that you play Craps and place pass line bets.
††This probability is in fact about 0.93773.
¶More precisely, we should say that about 94% of the players will win $1000 and about 6% will lose—each, $20,000.

average, the Casino will pay about $94,000 to the winners and collect about $120,000 from the losers. Hence, the Casino will have a nice profit of about $26,000.

Of course, when the probability of success is about 94/100, you are practically certain that you will reach your goal. You should not believe, however, that you can "put" $20,000 in your pocket and then, each time you need $1000, fly to Las Vegas or Atlantic City and get the money at the Craps tables! Easy calculations show that the probability of winning *twice in a row* with the "method" described above is

$$\frac{94}{100} \times \frac{94}{100} = \text{about } 0.88.$$

The chance of success is still considerable, but smaller than that of winning $1000 in one try. If you try the same "method" *ten times in a row*, the chance of winning each time is only about 0.52. And remember: If you lose once, you lose $20,000.

IV

One other interesting result is the following. *John starts with $1000, places pass line bets and stops when he either loses his $1000 capital or when he wins $1000.* Hence, he stops playing as soon as he doubles his initial $1000 capital. In this case, we can show that John's probability of success* is about 43/100. Hence, about 43% of the players who proceed this way will double their capital. About 57% of these players will be ruined.

Observe that in the above examples we assumed that John played Craps and placed bets on the pass line. The results would have been different if John had participated in some other game. For instance, assume John has $1000, makes $100 bets on red at a Roulette table and stops when he either makes $100 or loses his starting capital. In this case, we can show, using the

*We assume that John places $100 bets.

gambler's ruin formula, that the probability of winning $100 is about 85/100. This is smaller than the probability of winning $100 when making pass line bets. The decrease in the probability of success is due to the fact that the player has a better chance of winning a pass line bet than a bet on red at a Roulette table.

We close this section with the famous *gambler's ruin formula*. Assume that John participates in a game in which the probability of winning a bet is p. The probability of losing is $q = 1 - p$.* He makes bets of equal amounts. His capital is equal to C bets. He wants to win W bets. He will play until he either wins W bets or loses his capital C.** In this case, the probability that he is ruined (that is, the probability that he loses the capital C) is

$$P_{\text{ruin}} = \frac{1 - (\frac{p}{q})^W}{1 - (\frac{p}{q})^{W+C}}.$$

The probability of success (that is, the probability that he wins W bets) is

$$P_{\text{success}} = 1 - P_{\text{ruin}}.$$

That is,

$$P_{\text{success}} = \frac{(\frac{p}{q})^W - (\frac{p}{q})^{W+C}}{1 - (\frac{p}{q})^{W+C}}.$$

Here we notice that if the amount you desire to win is a large number of bets, then no matter what capital you have, the chance of success is quite negligible. To clarify this, assume that you place pass line bets of $10 and that you would like to win

---

*We assume $p \neq q$.
**In the case discussed in the first example, we have $p = 976/1980$, $q = 1004/1980$, $C = 10$ and $W = 1$. In this case, $p/q =$ about 0.97211.

$4500. Hence, you want to win 450 bets. The ruin formula given above shows that this is almost impossible. In fact, in this case, the chance of success is smaller than 1/1,000,000, *no matter how much money you have.* Similar conclusions hold for all other games in which the House has an advantage. This is why Casinos do not go broke. One could say that the phenomenal growth of gambling areas such as Las Vegas, Atlantic City, Reno, etc., is "a monument" raised to the gambler's ruin formula.

GAMBLING SYSTEMS

Roughly speaking, a gambling system of the type we consider here is a set of rules according to which the player bets in a sequence of plays. In most systems, the size of the bet made on a certain play depends on the previous outcomes. For instance, the player may decide to start with a one-unit bet, to double the bet in case of a loss and to return to a one-unit bet in case of a win.

Have such systems any value? To answer such a question, we need more information about the game in which the system is being used and about the gambler's goal. In any case, if we bet on plays which form an "independent sequence"* and if the payoff at the end of a play does not depend on the previous outcomes, then we can prove "mathematically" that no gambling system can affect our percent advantage or disadvantage.** This means, in particular, that an advantageous game remains advantageous and that a disadvantageous game remains disadvantageous, no matter what gambling system we use. We observe, however, that systems might affect the duration of play and the probabilities of winning or losing certain amounts. We shall return to this matter later in this section and in the next and final section of this Chapter.

---

*This means that the outcome of a play in the sequence is not affected in any way by the outcomes of the other plays. This is the case, for example, when we place a sequence of bets in the game of Craps or Roulette. The dice and the Roulette wheel have no memory (J. Bertrand) and, one might say, no heart either.

**The percent advantage or disadvantage is computed with respect to the total amount *expected* to be waged in such a sequence.

Below are described some of the most popular gambling systems, as well as some which are not so well known.

The Double-up System

The most popular gambling system is the *Double-up system*. Its simplicity is one of the main reasons for its popularity. The gambler using this system starts with a one-unit bet, doubles the bet after each loss and starts all over again after each win. It is relatively easy to see that every sequence of plays ending with a win brings the player a profit of one unit.

Assume, for example, that Jack plays Craps, makes pass line bets and decides to use the *Double-up system*. He starts betting one unit, say a $5 chip, on the pass line. If he wins, he makes $5. If he loses, he will place a two-unit bet (that is, $10) on the pass line. If he loses this bet, he will place a four-unit bet on the pass line. If he loses again, he will place an eight-unit bet (that is, $40) on the pass line. If he wins now, he will receive $40. Observe that Jack made the following bets:

one-unit (loss), two-unit (loss), four-unit (loss), eight-unit (win).

Before he placed the eight-unit bet, Jack was losing seven units; that is, $35. With the eight-unit bet, he won eight units. This compensates the seven units loss and *gives him one unit (that is, $5) overall profit.*

Note that Jack risked

$$15 \text{ units } (15 = 1 + 2 + 4 + 8)$$

in all to win a $5 unit.

He could have lost the eight-unit bet as well. All right, some gamblers will say, even if Jack loses the eight-unit bet, can't he double up again, that is, place a *sixteen-unit* bet? If he wins now, he has lost

$$1 + 2 + 3 + 4 + 8 = 15 \text{ units,}$$

and gained sixteen units, for a net profit of one unit. And even if Jack loses the sixteen-unit bet, can't he double up again and *again*? He must win sometime! This method must be fool proof!

Unfortunately for the player, this method is not fool proof. It is true that the player who continues to place bets must win sometime (with probability 1). However, in practice, one cannot increase the bets over a certain limit. Assume, for instance, that you are in a plush Casino and play Craps at a $2000-maximum table. If you start with a $5 bet, lose nine times in a row and double after each loss, your tenth bet must be $2560. And this is a bet you are not allowed to make.* Don't believe that you cannot lose nine times in a row! Remember the "winning streaks" encountered at the MGM and Desert Inn in Las Vegas, described in Chapter 1. "Losing streaks" of similar length have an even higher probability of occurrence.

We shall return to the Double-up system in the next section of this Chapter.

The Double-up system is also known as the *Martingale* or *Geometric progression system*.

The D'Alembert System

One other popular system is the *D'Alembert system*. The gambler using this system starts with a one-unit bet, increases the bet by one unit after each loss and decreases the bet by one unit after each win (when the previous bet was higher than one unit). A sequence of bets placed according to this rule shows a profit whenever the amount of the next bet is one unit (in fact, it might show a profit even earlier).

The player may continue to bet in the manner described above until the next bet is a one-unit bet. A more conservative variant is to start all over again with a one-unit bet as soon as the sequence of plays shows a profit.

---

*If you are allowed to make bets as high as you want, and if you lose 20 times in a row, your next bet must be $111,616,000.

Assume, for example, that Jack decides to make pass line bets and to use the D'Alembert system. He starts by betting $5. If he loses, his next bet will be $10. If he loses again, his next bet will be $15. If he wins now, his next bet will be $10. If he also wins this two-unit bet, he will have, for this sequence of plays, a profit equal to $10.

Observe that it takes many more losses to reach the maximum bet limit when you use the D'Alembert system than when you use the Double-up system. This is one of the main differences between these two systems.

The D'Alembert system is also known as the *Pyramid, Seesaw* or *Arithmetic progression* system.

The Cancellation System

To use this system, Jack starts by writing a sequence of numbers; for example,

$$2, 1, 3, 6, 5, 7.$$

Then his first bet will be equal to the sum of the first and last number in the sequence. Hence, in the case we consider here, his first bet is a nine-unit bet. If he wins, he deletes the numbers 2 and 7, obtains the sequence

$$1, 3, 6, 5,$$

and bets now the sum of the first and last numbers in this new sequence. Hence, he places a six-unit bet. If he loses the nine-unit bet, he writes the number 9 to the right of 7 in the original sequence, obtains the sequence

$$2, 1, 3, 6, 5, 7, 9$$

and places as a bet the sum of the first and last number in this sequence. Hence, he places an eleven-unit bet.

Jack continues this way, until, *hopefully,* all the numbers in the original sequence are deleted. In this case, *Jack will have a profit equal to the sum of all numbers in the original sequence;*

that is, a profit of 24 units. If the unit was a $5 chip, he would have made $120.

Notice that Jack always bets the sum of the first and last numbers in "the sequence determined by the previous outcomes."* Also observe that it might very well happen that Jack will never succeed in deleting all or most of the numbers in his original sequence.

It might also happen that the outcomes are so that the original sequence "increases." In this case, Jack will have a loss.

A "bad" sequence of outcomes might require "a next bet" higher than the maximum bet allowed in the game Jack is playing. How quickly such a limit is reached depends, of course, on the numbers written in the original sequence and on the outcomes produced in the game.

The Cancellation system is also known as the *Labouchere system*.

The Oscar-Wilson System

This gambling system was described for the first time in Wilson's *The Casino Gambler's Guide*.[30] When using this system, Jack proceeds as follows: He starts by betting one unit. Whenever he loses, the next bet is the same as before. Whenever he wins, the next bet is larger by one unit, except when such a bet might produce a profit of more than one unit. In this case, the bet is adjusted so that, in case of a win, the profit is exactly one unit. Whenever a profit of one unit is achieved, Jack starts anew with a one-unit bet.

Direct probability calculations corresponding to this system seem to be very complicated.[29] Computer simulations[30] done by Julian Braun show that, if you play Craps and make pass line bets, then the chance that a sequence of outcomes leads to a bet larger than the maximum bet allowed is about

$$\frac{1}{4250}.$$

The average loss for such a sequence is about $13,100.

*If this sequence contains only one number, say 6, the player makes a six-unit bet.

In these calculations, the bet unit is $1 and the maximum bet allowed is $500.

The "Bet on 7" System

This is a system I learned from a lady gambler in Reno, Nevada. We shall call her Mary. She liked to play Craps and place bets on 7, as indicated in the diagram in Table 6. Remember that a bet on 7 is paid 4 to 1 in case of a win.

The numbers in the first line in Table 6 represent the *ranks* of the dice rolls. The numbers in the second line represent the amounts of the corresponding bets. The table shows, for example, that Mary placed a one-unit bet before the fourth roll. She placed a two-unit bet before the sixth roll.

If the game develops as described in the third row, then Mary loses the first two bets and wins the third. Her total profit is two units. If the game proceeds as described in the fifth row, then Mary loses the first four bets and wins the fifth. The fifth bet is a two-unit bet. In this case, Mary has a profit of four units.

After every win, Mary starts all over again with a one-unit bet. Mary has a profit for every sequence of plays which ends with a win. Of course, Mary may lose, but only if 7 is not produced in *seven successive rolls*. In this case, she will lose

11 units $(11 = 1 + 1 + 1 + 1 + 2 + 2 + 3)$.

Table 6.

	1	2	3	4	5	6	7	
	1	1	1	1	2	2	3	PROFIT
1st row	W							4
2nd row	L	W						3
3rd row	L	L	W					2
4th row	L	L	L	W				1
5th row	L	L	L	L	W			4
6th row	L	L	L	L	L	W		2
7th row	L	L	L	L	L	L	W	4

When using this system, Mary has a probability of about

$$0.72092$$

of ending a sequence of plays with a profit. Hence, she will have a profit almost three-quarters of the time. The other times she will lose 11 units.

General Remarks

I shall mention two more "gambling systems" which, quite surprisingly, are used by many players.

For example, there are players who wait close to a Craps table until they see that their fellow players lose several pass line bets in a row. Then they rush and place a pass line bet. These players believe, of course, that by proceeding this way they increase their chances of winning. *These beliefs are completely erroneous.*

Unfortunately, this kind of fallacy is encountered not only in gambling, but also in everyday life.

One other "system" (which in a certain sense is opposite to the one mentioned above) is followed by the players who search for "hot Craps tables"* and place bets only on such tables. One "less ambitious" player, who is also the author of a book on gambling, even suggests that when you cannot find a "hot table" you should look at least for a "warm one." *This is complete nonsense.* What would the believers in "hot tables" do if Casinos installed refrigeration units under their Craps tables?!

These last two "systems" do not affect in any way the chances of winning or losing. What happened in the last 21 (or 41 or 101) rolls of the dice has *absolutely no bearing* on what will happen next.

It makes sense to say that a table *was* hot, when most of the players at that table were winning. It does not make any sense to assume that because most players at a table were winning, they and other gamblers entering the game will continue to win.

---

*In gambling jargon, a table is "hot" when the players at that table are winning.

It is important to realize that if, for example, you toss a coin ten times in a row and obtain only heads, the chances of obtaining a head or a tail on the eleventh toss are the *same* as on the first toss.

The player who places pass line bets only after several such bets were lost by other players believes that if you obtained heads ten times in a row, then the chance of obtaining a tail on the eleventh toss is increased. The players who search for "hot tables" behave as if they believe that if you obtained heads ten times in a row, heads will continue to be tossed more often than tails. As we have already said, such beliefs are completely mistaken.

Many erroneous ideas concerning games of chance, and probability in general, are often spread by popular TV programs. I remember when, some time ago, a TV show presented a "female android"* who was making quick calculations based on the previous outcomes of the rolls at a Craps table and, this way, was predicting the next outcomes. More recently, on a TV show which displays good looking women, a "professor" with a small calculator was predicting the outcomes of the rolls of the dice at a Craps table in a major Las Vegas Casino. *Nobody*, with or without a computer, can perform such feats.

I close this section by observing that in favorable games (as, for instance, in Blackjack, when played skillfully), the Kelly betting system[15] is useful. It would be too complicated to describe this system here.

MORE ON THE DOUBLE-UP SYSTEM

Here are a few more remarks concerning the Double-up system. As in the previous section, assume that Jack makes pass line bets at a $2000-maximum bet Craps table, uses the Double-up system and starts with a $5 bet.

If he loses nine times in a row, his next bet must be $2560. This is a bet he cannot make.

Observe that either Jack loses nine times in a row or he ends the sequence of bets with a win, and therefore with a $5 profit.

*That is, a robot with the appearance of a woman.

The probability that Jack loses nine times in a row is about 1/451. We deduce that the probability that he ends a sequence of plays with a win is about 450/451 (= 1 − 450/451); that is, about

$$\frac{998}{1000}.$$

Hence, *Jack is practically certain to make $5 when he starts a sequence of bets and uses the Double-up system.*

Of course, Jack must have enough capital to support a sequence of losses. Note that, if he loses nine times in a row, the total loss will be $2555. This is quite a large sum to risk for winning $5, even when you know that the chance of losing it is exceedingly small.

On the other hand, it is almost certain that Jack will try to win more than $5. Hence, he will start a new sequence of bets again and again.

The probability that he wins $100 without encountering a disastrous sequence of nine losses in a row is about

$$\frac{956}{1000}. \quad *$$

Is this a better result than the one John obtained by the method described in the example I, p. 127? At first it might seem so, since John's probability of winning $100 was only 9/10. Observe, however, that Jack risked $2555 with his method, while John risked $1000.

Of course, when you use the Double-up system, you might be able to continue to play without brining new capital into the game, even after you encounter a disastrous sequence of nine losses in a row. For example, assume that 15 sequences in a row end with a $5 gain and that the next sequence is a disastrous one. In this case, you lost $2555, but you still have $75 which

---

*The probability of winning $500 this way is about 80/100. The probability of winning $5000 is only about 11/100.

you may use to try to reach your goal. Of course, you must also recover the $2555 loss.

Before closing this section, one more case should be considered. Assume John has $1000, does not want to risk any other additional capital and wants to make $100. He places pass line bets at a Craps table and decides to play "boldly." This means, here, that each time he makes a bet he wagers the *smallest* of the following amounts: *either* 1) all the money remaining in his possession, *or* 2) an amount which will bring him a profit of $100 in case of a win. For example, John starts with a $100 bet. If he loses, he will place a $200 bet. If he loses this bet also, he will place a $400 bet on the pass line. Notice that if he loses again he cannot continue to use the Double-up system, since all the money he still has is $300. In this case, John will bet $300. If he wins, he will bet $500. If he wins again, he has attained his $100 profit target.

Calculations show that "bold" play gives John a better chance of success than the methods previously described.*

*The conclusion is the same in the case of other unfavorable games.

Bibliography

1. H. Asbury, *The Sucker's Progress (An Informal History of Gambling in America from the Colonies to Canfield),* Dodd, Mead & Co., New York, 1938.
2. N. Bourbaki, *Theorie des Ensembles, Fascicule de Resultats,* Hermann, Paris, 1958.
3. B. H. Brown, "Probabilities in the Game of Shooting Craps," *Am. Math. Monthly* **26:**351, 1919.
4. D. R. Byrkit, *Elementary Business Statistics,* D. Van Nostrand, New York, 1979.
5. C. Cotton, *The Compleat Gamester, First Edition,* London, 1674. Reprinted 1970 (Barre, Massachusetts, Imprint Society).
6. F. N. David, *Games, Gods and Gambling,* Hafner, New York, 1962.
7. L. E. Dubins and L. J. Savage, *How to Gamble if You Must,* McGraw-Hill, New York, 1965.
8. W. R. Eadington (Ed.), *Gambling and Society,* Charles C. Thomas, Springfield, Illinois, 1976.
9. R. A. Epstein, *The Theory of Gambling and Statistical Logic,* Academic Press, New York, 1977.
10. G. L. Fraikin, *Inside Nevada Gambling,* Exposition Press, New York, 1962.
11. S. Frey, *Dice Games,* Hart, New York, 1975.
12. B. Friedman, *Casino Games,* Golden Press, New York, 1973.

13. Galileo Galilei, *Sopra le scoperte dei dadi,* Opere, Firenze, Barbera 8, 1898.
14. V. L. Graham and C. Ionescu Tulcea, *A Book on Casino Gambling, Second Edition,* Van Nostrand Reinhold, New York, 1978.
15. C. Ionescu Tulcea, *Betting Systems* **I**, Technical Report, 1979.
16. M. G. Kendall and J. D. Murchland, "Statistical Aspects of the Legality of Gambling," *J. Royal Statistical Society* **127***(Pt. 3, Series A)*:359–391, 1964.
17. *Las Vegas Review J.,* October 1, 1964.
18. H. G. Levinson, *Chance, Luck and Statistics,* Dover, New York, 1963.
19. M. MacDougall, *MacDougall on Dice and Cards,* Coward-McCann, New York, 1944.
20. L. E. Maistrov, *Probability Theory (A Historical Sketch),* Academic Press, New York, 1974 (translation by S. Kotz of the 1967 Russian Edition).
21. P. R. de Montmort, *Essay d'Analyse sur les Jeux de Hasard,* J. Quillau, Paris, 1708 (may be found in the Library of Congress, Washington D.C., rare books collection).
22. M. Nosal, *Basic Probability and Applications,* W. B. Saunders, Philadelphia, Pennsylvania, 1977.
23. E. S. Pearson and M. G. Kendall (Eds.), *Studies in the History of Statistics and Probability,* Charles Griffin, London, 1970.
24. Ed Reid and O. Demaris, *The Green Felt Jungle,* Pocket Books, New York, 1964.
25. J. Scarne, *Scarne on Dice,* Stackpole, Harrisburg, Pennsylvania, 1974.
26. E. O. Thorp, *Beat the Dealer,* Random House, New York, 1966.
27. E. O. Thorp, "Optimal Gambling Systems for Favorable Games," *Review of the International Statistical Institute* **37***,37*:273–293, 1969.

28. D. Wiley, *Understanding Gambling Systems,* GBC Press, Las Vegas, Nevada, 1975.

29. A. N. Wilson, "Problem, Proposed by A. N. Wilson," *Am. Math. Monthly* **29:**570–571, 1962.

30. A. N. Wilson, *The Casino Gambler's Guide,* Harper and Row, New York, 1965.

Index

Index